C000178888

Bare Britain

What to do when you've nothing on

Written by
Nick Mayhew-Smith and Mike Charles

Senior artworker
Emete Friddle

Produced under contract by
Wardour Communications Ltd

We welcome feedback from readers. Reports of suitable additional entries and updates on current listings are particularly welcome for inclusion in later editions. We thank you in advance for all such information.

info@lifestyle-press.co.uk

You can buy new copies online at:
www.barebritain.com
Or send a cheque with your name and address (UK only) for £14.95 (includes £2 post and packing) to:
Lifestyle Press Ltd
PO Box 1087
Bristol BS48 3YD
These prices valid to June 2007, subject to availability.

Cover picture: Slapton Beach, Devon

We would like to thank the many organisations and people who have helped and encouraged the production of this book, particularly Charlie Simonds, Andrew Welch, Malcolm Boura, Suzanne Piper, Iain Thornber, David Martin, Mick Goody, Przemek and Joanna.

First published in June 2005 by Lifestyle Press Ltd, PO Box 1087, Bristol BS48 3YD, UK.

info@lifestyle-press.co.uk

www.barebritain.com

Copyright © Lifestyle Press Ltd 2005

All rights reserved. No part of this book may be translated, reproduced or transmitted in any form or by any means, electronic, mechanical, photocopying or otherwise, without the prior permission of the publisher, except for brief extracts for inclusion in critical articles and reviews.

British Library Cataloguing-in Publication Data. A catalogue record for this book is available from the British Library.

Although the publisher of this book has made every effort to ensure that the information was correct at the time of going to press, the publisher does not assume and hereby disclaims any liability to any party for any loss or damage caused by errors, omissions or misleading information. The nature of the guide is such that the content may quickly become outdated. Neither the authors, publishers or distributors of this guide can be held responsible should nudity cause you to be arrested or prosecuted for any offence.

ISBN 0-9544767-2-7

Association of Publishing Agencies
ADVANCING CUSTOMER PUBLISHING

Produced in partnership with British Naturism

It's surprising how something so simple could be so enjoyable. But it's really true – there's nothing quite like running naked into the sea for making you feel good about life.

This book is designed to show you how, where and why so many people are taking the simple step of swimming and sunbathing in their birthday suits.

Bare Britain was compiled in partnership with British Naturism, the UK's national organisation for naturists, to give the best possible picture of the country's bare bathing opportunities.

With more than 100 clubs and dozens of beaches, we have uncovered the country from Aberdeen to Anglesey and Kent to Cornwall.

Find out what people near you are doing when they've nothing on.

British Naturism 6-7

How to use this book 8-9

Bare beach basics 10-15
What to expect **12-13**
Beaches index **14-15**

South West beaches 16-33
Cornwall, Devon, Isles of Scilly

South coast beaches 34-55
Dorset, Hampshire, Isle of Wight, West Sussex,
East Sussex, Kent

East coast beaches 56-65
Essex, Suffolk, Norfolk, Lincolnshire, Yorkshire,
Northumberland

North West beaches 66-69
Cumbria

Scotland beaches 70-75
Arran, Jura, the Highlands

Wales beaches 76-85
Anglesey, Gwynedd, West Glamorgan, Vale of Glamorgan

Ireland beaches 86-93
Counties Dublin, Wicklow, Wexford, Kerry, Sligo

Best bares 94-95
Our selection of the best UK beaches and clubs

Holidays au naturel 96-111
European options **98-99**
10 best bare beaches worldwide **100-102**
Fully naturist resorts **104-106**
Spas and saunas in the UK **108**
UK naturist holidays **110-111**

www.barebritain.com

Bare places basics 112-117

Bare places index **116-117**

South West clubs 118-127

Bath/Bristol, Cornwall, Devon, Dorset, Gloucs, Somerset, Wiltshire

South East clubs 128-143

Berkshire, Buckinghamshire, East Sussex, Hampshire, Isle of Wight, Kent, Oxfordshire, Surrey, West Sussex

Eastern clubs 144-159

Bedfordshire, Cambridgeshire, Essex, Hertfordshire, Norfolk, Suffolk

Midlands clubs 160-165

Birmingham, Leicestershire, Lincolnshire, Northamptonshire, Nottinghamshire, Shropshire, Staffordshire, Warwickshire

Yorkshire clubs 166-169

East Yorkshire, North Yorkshire, South Yorkshire, West Yorkshire

North West clubs 170-177

Cheshire, Cumbria, Greater Manchester, Lancashire, Merseyside

North East clubs 178-179

Newcastle upon Tyne

Wales clubs 180-183

Gwynedd, Monmouthshire, Pembrokeshire, West Glamorgan

Scotland/Ireland clubs 184-187

Edinburgh, Loch Lomond, Glasgow, Aberdeen, Tayside, Dumfries and Galloway, Belfast

National clubs 188-191

Bare facts 192-200

Bare-friendly travel agents **194-195**
Holiday and travel information **196-197**
Naturist reading **198-199**
List of advertisers **200**

British Naturism, the natural choice

If the places in this book appeal to you, then why not join British Naturism? We are the national organisation for all bare-minded people in the UK, helping thousands of members get the most out of this wonderful pastime. Here are just some of the benefits of taking the simple step of joining us:

- A free copy of our superb colour magazine BN. Each quarterly issue is packed with news, holiday features, club and swim listings, advertising and photography.
- Support for all genuine naturist activity. We give you free personal accident insurance at any approved club or location, and work hard to protect and promote everyone's freedom to enjoy naturism in the UK.
- Free holiday advice from our team of holiday advisors.
- A free International Naturist Federation (INF) card, which you can use in many holiday resorts and clubs worldwide.
- Discounts on SeaFrance ferries, Green Flag recovery, and National and Dixons' car rental.

BN has been working for a long time to promote UK naturism. It was created in 1964 by the merger of two societies that had promoted naturism since UK naturism began in the 1930s. More recently, we successfully lobbied the government to change a new law on sexual offences, ensuring that naturist activity is now an accepted part of modern Britain. With your help we will continue our work so future generations can enjoy bare bathing just as much as we do today.

British Naturism is run mainly by volunteers with a staffed central office in Northampton. There are more than 150 clubs and swims affiliated to BN – even more than the dozens included in this book – and we are busy encouraging the establishment of yet more.

If you like the sound of us, we'd love to welcome you into our naturist world. It is easy to join:

- Sign up online at www.british-naturism.org.uk
- Email for more info: headoffice@british-naturism.org.uk
- Write to us at 30-32 Wycliffe Road, Northampton NN1 5JF
- Call us on 01604 620361

Jump in and join

the naturist world

B N

British Naturism

How to use Bare Britain

Before you bare

Given the huge choice of venues and public tolerance of nudity in the right context, anyone can enjoy a carefree bare bathing experience in the UK without worrying about offending others. But there are limits and a tradition of bare bathing can start or stop at any given location for a range of reasons. If you are in doubt about whether it is suitable to strip, we have provided substantial tourist and naturist contact information throughout the guide to help keep you up to date with the latest situation. Our website www.barebritain.com includes any significant updates about the venues listed in these pages.

Photographs

It goes without saying that you should expect to visit a bare beach or naturist club without worry about cameras. The pictures in this book, while attempting to depict the beaches listed accurately, have all been edited to ensure the anonymity of general beach users. You may see the same bottom appearing in quite a few shots, but we have tried to reflect the fact that literally anybody, of any age, race or body type is able to try the simple freedom of going bare.

Newer and nuder

There are so many places to enjoy genuine naturism in the UK, even more than we have listed in this book. We are publishing full updates to this guide on our website www.barebritain.com. And above all we are including your feedback. We are keen to make sure our guides are as accurate and as inclusive as possible when it comes to covering the bare bathing world. If you have any reports, pictures or suggestions for future editions of either Bare Britain or our sister title Bare Beaches, please get in touch with us either by email:

info@lifestyle-press.co.uk

Or write to:

Lifestyle Press Ltd, PO Box 1087, Bristol BS48 3YD

Simply being at one with nature: you can enjoy it just as much alone as in a crowd. Pictures show **Pevors Farm** naturist holiday centre (opposite above, see page 153) and the UK's most popular beach at **Studland** (opposite bottom, see page 38). Picture above supplied by Pevors Farm

At its most simple, being naked on a beach is the most peaceful and innocent way to enjoy the beautiful British coastline. *Bare Britain* was written to reflect the fact that nude beaches are now a regular and accepted part of the seaside experience.

Most of the beaches in this book have a long tradition of bare bathing. And we hope this guide will help that tradition continue long into the future. The tips on this page are little more than good manners or common sense, and are chosen to give a fully rounded view of the UK bare beach experience.

Safe in the sunshine

However harmless it may seem, and however good it may feel, sun on skin can lead to serious health problems. Exposing yourself to too much sun is never a good idea as it can cause burning and trigger various types of skin cancer. To enjoy fully the freedom of sunbathing and swimming outside naked, it is essential to protect your body from the sun's harmful rays.

When we step into the sunshine for the first time, most of us can withstand the sun's rays without any sun protection for a maximum of 20 minutes before burning. So you need to choose a suitable sun cream that offers the correct European sun protection factor (SPF) for your skin type. For example, if you choose a sun cream with SPF 12, you have protection that allows you to stay in the sun 12 times longer than you could without protection, before burning.

Remember also to stay out of the sun between 11am and 3pm, when the sun is at its fiercest, and wear a sun hat.

Finally, do check yourself regularly for any moles that bleed, itch, change shape or look unusual; even red spots or ulcers that never fully heal can be a form of cancer. Don't hesitate to see your doctor: skin cancers can often be fully cured with simple treatment, and the earlier you get them sorted the better.

Skin care and cancer information
www.skincancer.org
www.cancerresearchuk.org/sunsmart
www.skincancerfacts.org.uk

Hassle

If you're used to baring all on a Spanish or French beach you can find places and times when British beaches are just as free and easy. But in a few places even long-term naturists complain about the level of disturbance from other visitors. Some beaches are better than others and we've tried to give some guidance about where it is a particular issue.

It makes no difference if someone ruining your day is a clothed or naked beach user. If you feel people looking at you, sitting too close, approaching you or in some way trying to attract your attention, it may well take the edge off what should be a lovely and relaxing experience. If someone is being a pest, you can ask them to stop it, threaten to report them to the police or landowner, or actually report them. Mobile phones, especially those with cameras, are a good way to record any problems.

And if you want to know what behaviour is acceptable on a nude beach – it's exactly the same as an ordinary beach, apart from the lack of swimming costumes.

Finding the beach

By their very nature many of the best beaches for baring all are remote, and in a few instances hard to find. There may not be many people around to ask for directions, but those you do meet have a good chance of sharing your interest in the place.

Every beach listing includes full directions for getting there. We include general location maps to help you find the beach on your own road atlas. The map references are based on the Ordnance Survey grid. For accurate navigation the Landranger series 1:50 000 (1.25 inches = 1 mile) and the Explorer series 1:25 000 (2.5 inches = 1 mile) are the most popular leisure maps.

Law in the raw

It would be a strange country that made it illegal simply to be naked. Certainly Britain does not have a law that bans being naked per se, and the law was changed in 2003 to allow for genuine naturist and bare bathing activity. In England and Wales, it is only an offence to expose yourself if you intend to cause alarm or distress. If you mind your own business and take reasonable steps to ensure you don't confront other beach users, then there shouldn't be any problems with a peaceful and innocent pastime such as bare bathing.

We have tried where possible to explain how well established bare bathing is at the beaches in our book. About a dozen UK beaches are called 'official' beaches. This means the local authority has designated them as recognised places for baring all. British Naturism gives free personal accident insurance to all its members visiting approved naturist locations; see pages 6-7 for more info.

Note that the laws in Scotland are under review at the time of writing and you should check the current situation if in any doubt about your right to bare all on a certain beach. Bare beaches listed in the Irish Republic section are all unofficial and discretion is always advised. Consideration for others is the best way to ensure greater tolerance and understanding of naked bathing.

The excellent Naturist UK FactFile website www.nuff.org.uk carries updates about most of the sites listed in this book. More beach information is available from British Naturism www.british-naturism.org.uk

Acknowledgements
The beach listings were compiled with the help of the **Naturist UK FactFile** website (www.nuff.org.uk), the **British Naturism** website (www.british-naturism.org.uk), the **Irish Naturist Association** (www.esatclear.ie/~irishnaturist/) and individual contributions from many kind naturists around the UK and the Irish Republic

Places to stay
All accommodation listed near the bare beaches is **not** naturist or linked to naturism at all, unless specifically stated otherwise. It has been included to help find local places to stay. The organisations on pages 196-7 can provide more ideas

Bare Beaches

South West   **16-33**
Cornwall, Isles of Scilly, Devon

South coast   **34-55**
Dorset, Hampshire, Isle of Wight, W Sussex, E Sussex, Kent

East coast   **56-65**
Essex, Suffolk, Norfolk, Lincolnshire, Yorkshire, Northumberland

North West   **66-69**
Cumbria

Scotland   **70-75**
Arran, Jura, the Highlands

Wales   **76-85**
Anglesey, Gwynedd, West Glamorgan, Vale of Glamorgan

Ireland   **86-93**
Counties Dublin, Wicklow, Wexford, Kerry, Sligo

Embracing the south coast. Picture by
Charlie Simonds of naturist film maker
Parafotos (www.parafotos.co.uk)

South West

Sillery Sands

East of Lynmouth, North Devon   *Map ref: SS739498*
An unspoilt bare beach which stretches for more than half a mile
below dramatic cliffs on the edge of the Exmoor National Park.
It's an **escapist's paradise** perfect for just sitting, listening to
the waves and watching the sun sink slowly over the bay. The
shoreline consists of pebbles and coarse sand. With a long
tradition of nude bathing the few swimsuited visitors and the
bare ones happily co-exist.

Travel east from Lynmouth on the A39 coast road for just over
a mile as it climbs **Countisbury Hill**. A small layby on the
right-hand side (and about a third of the way up the hill) is the
starting point for the footpath which leads to the beach. The
path is steep but well maintained by the National Trust. The
walk down takes around 15 minutes, but allow a little longer to
climb back up.

The historic **Sandpiper Inn**, perched on the hillside a further
half-mile beyond the layby towards Countisbury, provides
refreshments and comfortable rooms. Opposite the inn, the
National Trust's **Countisbury Cottage** sleeps four. **Channel
View Caravan and Camping Park**, approximately 3 miles
from the beach, boasts a David Bellamy Gold Conservation
Award. Tourist info: www.northdevon.com

Wild Pear Beach

East of Combe Martin, near Ilfracombe, north Devon
Map ref: SS580477
A delightfully sheltered cove of sand and rock, officially
recognised as a bare beach. The sea is normally crystal clear and
fresh water springs cascade down the surrounding slate cliffs.
Generally very quiet, which might be something to do with the
rather **challenging access**, which makes it best suited to those
with the agility of a mountain goat.

The nearest parking is half a mile away in Combe Martin (said
to be the village with the longest street in England – 2 miles).
Take the coast path from the back of the Foc'sle Inn which climbs
steeply towards Hangmans Hills. Continue past a covered resting
shelter and over the stile. The path down to the beach is then on
the left, but not well marked amongst the undergrowth. It
becomes steep and can be slippery as it zigzags down to the
shore. **Particular care** is required on the final descent.

As *Bare Britain* went to press, Wild Pear beach was officially

1 **Sillery Sands**
2 **Wild Pear Beach**

Sandpiper Inn
www.exmoor-sandpiper.co.uk
Tel: 01598 741263

Countisbury Cottage
www.nationaltrustcottages.co.uk
Tel: 0870 4584422

Channel View Caravan & Camping
www.channel-view.co.uk
Tel: 01598 753349

Devon and Cornwall have many of
England's finest beaches, with a large
choice of bare beaches all along the
coast. **Pednevounder** in Cornwall,
left, is rated among the very best by
bare beach lovers (see page 25)

Marsdens Cottages
www.marsdens.co.uk
Tel: 01271 813777

**West Challacombe Manor &
West Challacombe Cottage**
www.nationaltrustcottages.co.uk
Tel: 0870 4584422

Stowford Farm Meadows
www.stowford.co.uk
Tel: 01271 882476

**Newberry Farm Caravan and
Camping**
www.newberrycampsite.co.uk
Tel: 01271 882334
Fax: 01271 882880

Wheel Farm Cottages
www.wheelfarmcottages.co.uk
Tel: 01271 882100

Saunton Sands, by Charlie Simonds,
right, has plenty of space to bare, but
Polgaver beach, left, is now closed

closed due to winter storm damage to the access path. Check with the local Tourist Information Centre (tel: 01271 883319, email: mail@visitcombemartin.co.uk).

A choice of self-catering properties in and around Combe Martin is available from **Marsdens Cottages**. The National Trust has accommodation at **West Challacombe Manor** and **West Challacombe Cottage**. The well-equipped **Stowford Farm Meadows** Caravan and Camping Park was voted outright winner of the Best British Site award in 2004. The less commercial **Newberry Farm** Caravan and Camping is only five minutes' walk from Combe Martin beach, and also nearby eight cottages at **Wheel Farm** share an indoor pool for non-bare bathing. Tourist info: www.northdevon.com

Saunton Sands

West of Barnstaple, North Devon   *Map ref: SS444345*
A lovely 3-mile long expanse of sandy shoreline, popular with surfers. It extends from the village of Saunton to the estuaries of the rivers Taw and Torridge at the southern end. Backed by Braunton Burrows, a huge area of dunes recognised by UNESCO as Britain's first **Biosphere Reserve**, there is also a

golf course and a Ministry of Defence training area. **Discreet bare bathing** on the more remote parts of the beach and dunes, farthest from the access points, has historically been enjoyed for years. The sand is almost flat so a pleasant walk to the sea is on the cards at low tide. Although reports that the local authority is **unsupportive** cast a mild shadow over its nudist credentials, feedback from summer 2004 suggests the beach remains as pleasant as ever. Don't expect to find many other bare bathers.

Travel west from Barnstaple on the A361 to Braunton. In the centre of the village branch left on to the B3231 towards **Croyde**. In a little over 2 miles the beach car park at Saunton is on the left. A restaurant and snack bar operate in high season and the shore here gets very busy. Walk south down the beach, well away from the crowds, to discover a haven of tranquillity (apart from the occasional helicopter from nearby RAF Chivenor).

Luxury accommodation at the 4-star **Saunton Sands Hotel** provides unrivalled views down the beach. Nearer to Barnstaple, **Combrew Farm** has four tasteful cottages and a new indoor pool and sauna. **Marsdens Cottages** have lots of properties in Braunton and Saunton. **Lobb Fields** Caravan & Camping is less than 2 miles from Saunton Sands. Best fish and chips in the area are at Squires in Braunton – they've won lots of awards.

Flexbury

Near Bude, North Cornwall   *Map ref: SS200080*
A beautiful stretch of **rural coastline** backed by rocky cliffs and National Trust land. Plenty of sandy beach as the tide recedes, but care is needed at high tide, when some of the more remote spots may be cut off for a short time. Rocky outcrops provide **seclusion** for sunbathing as nature intended. In fine weather the beach has a small following of locals who take advantage of baring all at this attractive spot.

Apart from at high tide, it is possible to walk north from Bude along the shore for just over a mile to the bare area. Alternatively, drive through **Flexbury** and **Maer** along the local lanes to the car park above the beach at **Northcott Mouth**. From here it is a half-mile walk to the south. There is also a quiet beach to explore to the north of the car park in the direction of Sandy Mouth.

The **Brendon Arms** offers B&B in Bude and the company also has holiday apartments in the **Old Lifeboat House** in the town. Not far from the bare beach, the family-oriented **Bude Holiday Park**, at Maer, has mobile homes as well as camping and caravanning. Self-catering cottages at **Broomhill Manor** have non-naturist swimming pools, spa, sauna and solarium.

Tourist info: www.cornwalltouristboard.co.uk

1 **Saunton Sands**
2 **Flexbury**

Saunton Sands Hotel
www.sauntonsands.co.uk
Tel: 01271 890212

Combrew Farm
www.northdevonholidays.com
Tel: 01271 373834

Marsdens Cottages
www.marsdens.co.uk
Tel: 01271 813777

Lobb Fields Caravan & Camping
www.lobbfields.com
Tel: 01271 812090

The handy **NatCorn** website run by Keith Gordon has details of naturist beaches and clubs in Cornwall
www.natcorn.org.uk

Brendon Arms & Old Lifeboat House
www.brendonarms.co.uk
Tel: 01288 354542

Bude Holiday Park
www.chycor.co.uk/parks/bude
Tel: 0845 1301515

Broomhill Manor
www.broomhillmanor.co.uk
Tel: 01288 352940

1 The Strangles
2 Penhale Sands

Trevigue
www.trevigue.co.uk
Tel: 01840 230418 or 01840 230492

Combe Barton Inn
info@combebartoninn.com
Tel: 01840 230345

The Old Cider Press
www.theoldciderpress.co.uk
Tel: 020 8993 2628

**Lower Poulza Post Farm
(naturist)**
Jacobstowe, Bude, Cornwall EX23 0BX
Tel: 01566 781520 (6pm-9pm)

The Strangles, opposite top, has two areas used by bare bathers, separated by the rocky outcrop, depending on how busy the place gets at weekends. **Penhale Sands**, opposite below, always has plenty of space to relax or explore, making it well worth the walk to get there – but bring your day's supplies with you

The Strangles

Near Crackington Haven, North Cornwall   Map ref: SX131954
A hauntingly attractive beach and a favourite of **Thomas Hardy** more than 100 years ago. The pebble and shingle shore gives way to large sandy areas as the tide goes out. Relatively sheltered by high cliffs, the beach is undeveloped and attracts a mix of swimsuited and bare bathers. An influx of clothed visitors on peak weekends might make a short scramble over the low rocky outcrop at the north of the bay to the nudist cove, known as **Little Strand**, advisable. Take care not to get cut off at high tide.

Travel 8 miles south of Bude on the A39 coastal highway to **Wainhouse Corner**. Turn right onto the minor road signposted to Crackington Haven. The village is reached in just less than 3 miles. Take the lane heading south for a mile to the National Trust property of Trevigue, where there is roadside parking and the footpath to the beach. Follow the well-marked track and once down on the shore turn right for peace and seclusion.

High above the beach and nestled in a hollow on the cliffs, **Trevigue** provides B&B and self-catering accommodation. It also has a gourmet restaurant renowned for its wholesome fare. The **Combe Barton Inn** at Crackington Haven is recommended in the *2005 AA Pub Guide*. Three miles away, luxury self-catering is available at the 2-bedroomed **Old Cider Press**. The 17th century isolated National Trust **Elm Cottage** is to the south towards Boscastle. Popular **naturist** camping is on offer 5 miles from The Strangles at **Lower Poulza Post Farm**, with 40 secluded acres to explore on this working farm. Tourist info: www.cornwalltouristboard.co.uk

Penhale Sands

Perranporth, Cornwall   *Map ref: SW762575*
The wide open spaces of Penhale Sands are invitation enough to fling your clothes into the air and **streak joyously** towards the sea – but you might want to rest first after the long walk there. It is easy to find and much loved by bare bathers in the summer.

Nude use has long been accepted here – indeed clothed bathers are unlikely to come near given that the bare bathers have picked the **furthest spot** from the main town beach at Perranporth. The sea is very clean but as always take care in heavy surf.

There are some steep dunes behind the beach and when the tide is out plenty of pools and cliffs to explore around the headland. There is a coastal path running along the back of the beach but the area is so vast both sunbathers and walkers have **plenty of space** for themselves.

It's easy enough to find from Perranporth – simply walk about

www.barebritain.com

Southleigh Manor (naturist)
www.southleigh-manor.com
Tel: 01637 880938

Seiners' Arms
www.seinersarms.com
Tel: 01872 573118

The Perranporth Hotel
www.perranporth-hotel.co.uk
Tel: 01872 573234

Perranporth youth hostel
www.yha.org.uk/hostel/
                  hostelpages/91.html
Tel: 0870 770 5994

Penhale Sands has all the space in
the world, and interesting cliffs to
explore when the tide is out

1.5 miles along the beach to the far north end (right as you face
the sea), where the large headland ends this vast beach. You can
park a bit closer if you turn off to the north just before entering
Perranporth, down a minor road to the hamlet of **Mount** and **St
Pirans Oratory**. Walk to the site of the 6th century oratory,
which is now buried in the sands, and over the dunes to the
beach. St Piran, who gave Perranporth its name, is said to have
discovered tin smelting when a stone on his fire began to ooze
the metal.

About 10 miles away the lovely naturist holiday camp of
Southleigh Manor has everything a freedom-loving camper or
caravanner could want, but it does get booked up in busy times.
In Perranporth itself, non-naturist options include pubs such as
the **Seiners' Arms**, hotels such as **The Perranporth Hotel** and
a **youth hostel** with views towards the distant naturist beach.

Fishing Cove

Near Navax Point, north-east of Hayle, Cornwall
Map ref: SW596429
A delightful north-east facing sandy cove criss-crossed by
streams flowing into the sea. Bare bathers will delight in the

generally calm and sheltered sea. Other than in mid-summer the sun soon goes down behind the cliffs. **Grey seals** and **dolphins** can often be spotted off the beach and the area is a haven for cormorants, razorbills and oystercatchers. The famous Godrevy Lighthouse can be seen offshore by taking a short walk along the cliffs.

From Hayle take the B3301 towards **Gwithian** and **Portreath**. Travel through Gwithian and continue for a little over a mile and a half to a small National Trust car park located almost on the edge of the cliffs. Walk 200 yards to the west and take the path down to the cove below. Although quite steep it is not as difficult as it might first appear.

The nearest camping is at **Gwithian Farm** in the village of the same name. **Godrevy Park** Caravan Club is within 3 miles of the beach and close by the **Atlantic Coast** Touring and Camping Park has mobile homes for hire. For a contemporary designer B&B try **Seaview** in St Ives; it's not cheap but quite special. For more local information see www.gwithian.org.uk

Isles of Scilly

28 miles south-west of Land's End, Cornwall   Map ref: SV905105
An archipelago of 100 tiny islands, each less than three miles across. Only five of the islands are inhabited – St Mary's, Tresco, Bryher, St Martin's and St Agnes. Long hours of sunshine – the name 'Scilly Isles' means 'Sun Isles' – and near-deserted Caribbean-quality beaches make this a special destination for the **discerning but discreet** bare bather.

St Martin's has the very best soft white sand and is favoured for private au naturel sunning. The eastern end of Higher Town Bay on the south coast is usually quiet, otherwise walk across to Stony Porth (to the west of the Day Mark and St Martin's Head) on the opposite side of the island, or further west to Great Bay, described by the Tourist Board as simply the most perfect beach on the islands. Lawrence's Bay, on the south coast, has acres of white sand, with rock pools, sandy bars and lagoons.

Rushy Bay, near the southern

1 Fishing Cove
2 Scilly Isles

Gwithian Farm
www.gwithianfarm.co.uk
Tel: 01736 753127

Godrevy Park
www.caravanclub.co.uk
Tel: 01736 753100

Atlantic Coast Touring & Camping
www.chycor.co.uk/parks/atlantic_coast
Tel: 01736 752071

Seaview
www.seaview-stives.co.uk
Tel: 01736 798001

The sheltered **Fishing Cove**, below, is sunniest at the start of the day. Picture by Di and Dave Parsons

Pednevounder, opposite bottom, has a spectacular view towards Logan's Rock, a 70-tonne stone balanced on the top of an outcrop. White sands to rival the Caribbean on **St Martin's**, below, and secluded coves on **St Mary's**, bottom, are often empty enough for some unofficial bare bathing. Pictures on this page by Mike Gould

tip of **Bryher** is recommended and on **St Agnes**, head east across the tidal sandbar to **Gugh** for deserted nooks and crannies. Of the uninhabited islands, **Sampson** has some delightful scenery, particularly if you are lucky enough to find you have the island to yourself and can play Robinson Crusoe.

Lots of secluded coves are to be found on **St Mary's**, away from Hugh Town, the capital of the islands. Mike Gould, a regular naturist visitor to the Isles of Scilly, advises: "There are plenty of other places to discover, although you are unlikely to come across too many skinny dippers. Common sense is the key to an enjoyable and natural experience in this beautiful paradise."

Travel from the mainland to St Mary's by plane, helicopter or ferry. Crossings to the other islands are by local scheduled launches or water taxi. **Walking** is the most popular and often the only way to explore the islands. The tourist board website www.simplyscilly.co.uk has full details, or call in to any high street travel agent to arrange travel to St Mary's. The Ordnance Survey large-scale Explorer Map No 101 (1:25000) is recommended.

The tourist board website also has details of a wealth of places

to stay. The **St Martin's Hotel** on St Martin's is an exclusive and expensive establishment with a reputation for fine cuisine, while the **Polreath** guesthouse (4 diamonds) has ensuite rooms. Also on St Martin's there are six self-catering properties (3- and 4-star) and a campsite. On St Agnes, the **Turks Head**, 50 yards from the quayside, is the most southwesterly pub in Britain (*AA Pub Guide 2005* recommended), and offers B&B. However, most of the Scilly's accommodation is on St Mary's. The **Auriga** guesthouse is said to be very friendly.

Additional tourist info: www.scillyonline.co.uk and for the tourist board www.simplyscilly.co.uk (01720 422536).

Pednevounder

Near Treen, Cornwall   *Map ref: SW393223*

This uniquely beautiful cove nestles at the foot of spectacular cliffs, which make access tricky but the views sublime. A golden sandy bay with bright blue water awaits anyone making the tricky scramble down. The mix of clad and unclad bathers is about half and half – with just the sort of **laid back attitude** that would put even a first time bare bather entirely at ease.

The fine yellow sand, cyan waters and amazing rock formations in the bay could trick you into dreaming you're in the tropics, although a quick skinny dip in the sea will soon wake you up. The sands are almost completely covered at high tide, while at low tide there is a huge expanse of shallow water, sand banks and golden beach to thrill any bare-minded soul. It's one that came up time and again when we asked UK naturists to name the country's **most beautiful bare beach**.

Park in the pay and display car park at **Treen** and walk down the narrow lane past Treen campsite to the coastal path. Don't take this main path, but follow the path branching off it which goes much closer to the (very steep) cliffs. A third very narrow but well used path leads off this down the rocks to

1 Pednevounder, near Treen

St Martin's Hotel
www.stmartins.co.uk
Tel: 01720 422090

Polreath, St Martin's
www.polreath.com
Tel: 01720 422046

Turks Head, St Agnes
drat@turkshead.fslife.co.uk
Tel: 01720 422434

Auriga, St Mary's
www.simplyscilly.co.uk
aurigascilly@aol.com
Tel: 01720 422637

Treen campsite
Tel: 01736 810273

Porthcurno Hotel
www.porthcurnohotel.co.uk
Tel: 01736 810119

Wisteria Cottage
www.bedandbreakfastwestcornwall.co.uk
Tel: 01736 811021

**Carlyon Bay Caravan & Camping
(naturist section)**
www.carlyonbay.net
Tel: 01726 812735

Little Crugwallins (naturist)
www.littlecrug-naturism.co.uk
rupertadkins@onetel.com
Tel: 01726 63882

Natsun Naturist B&B (naturist)
www.nat-sun.co.uk
Tel: 07919 093746

Vault Beach, below, has a beautiful location and enough space for bare and clothed bathers to coexist.
Picture by Andrew Welch

Pednevounder. It becomes a **very steep scramble** for the last section but if you feel able to tackle it and can manage heights the rewards are well worth it.

Accommodation is heavily booked in the summer thanks to many local attractions including the **Minack open-air theatre** at Porthcurno and Land's End. Treen itself offers a regular **campsite** while a walk along the coastal path at Porthcurno is the eight-bedroom **Porthcurno Hotel**, which has rooms and also manages some local self-catering accommodation. Eighteenth century **Wisteria Cottage** B&B, 4 miles from Pednevounder, is not naturist either – but the owners are naturist-friendly.

Vault Beach

Gorran Haven, Cornwall   *Map ref: SX009407*
An unspoilt bay of coarse sand and fine gravel which faces south-east. In an area of outstanding natural beauty, it enjoys a fine reputation for bare bathing, with dressed and undressed happily coexisting. The nude end is towards **Dodman Point**, while swimsuited visitors tend to use the opposite side of the bay. There are no facilities so take refreshments and shade with you. Although the descent to the shore is fairly steep, it is **popular with families**.

From St Austell, take the B3273 to **Mevagissey**, which can be a traffic bottleneck in peak season. Continue south on the unclassified road to **Gorran Haven**, through the village and up the steep narrow lane to the National Trust car park at **Lamledra**. The footpath leads from here to the north-east end of Vault Beach. Walk along the sand to the south-west side to locate the bare area. For an alternative route to the bay follow the coast path from Gorran Haven.

Carlyon Bay Caravan and Camping Park is a 5-star family touring site near St Austell. It has a separate secluded field with eight pitches reserved for naturists (excluding August), and is about 12 miles from Vault Beach. Also nearby are three naturist self-catering cottages to rent at **Little Crugwallins** (see page 120). And in St Austell itself a B&B called **Natsun Naturist B&B** offers genuine naturist accommodation and has a secluded garden.

Among non-naturist options

are **Granny's**, **Bodrugan** and **Edgcumbe** – three National Trust cottages at Penare close to Vault Beach. Luxury self-catering is available at **Fort Cottage** (Rural Retreats) situated in a prominent position adjacent to Gorran Haven beach. The award-winning 5-star **Seaview International** Holiday Park complete with swimming pool is at nearby Boswinger, which is also the location for **Boswinger Youth Hostel** (for all ages!).

Downderry

East of Looe, Cornwall   *Map ref: SX330538*

A series of three bays to the east of Downderry village, where the second and third ones are ideal for sunbathing naturally. The third bay is also popular with gay visitors. The sand is fairly coarse but the pretty coves are **completely undeveloped** and provide good shelter when the weather is breezy. Numerous rocky outcrops provide seclusion, but care is needed to avoid being cut off at high tide. The naturist **Carbeil Holiday Park**, which opened in Easter 2005 and is only a 15-20 minute walk away, will no doubt attract more naturists to the beach.

From the **Tamar Bridge** at Plymouth travel 8 miles west on the A38 to the roundabout at Trerulefoot. Take the first exit and follow the A374 for 1.3 miles, before turning right on to the A382 (signposted Looe). In 2 miles, at **Hessenford**, turn left on to the B3247 and a further 3 miles on is Downderry. Parking is limited, although there is a small car park in the village. Walk east along the road out of the village and as it swings sharply left inland, drop down the short path to the beach in front. Walk along the sand (east) to the second bay, avoiding high tide to gain access. It should be possible to exit the naturist beach by scrambling up the steep cliff path at the back of the cove and following the track around the fields back to the road.

The naturist **Carbeil Holiday Park**, half a mile from the village, has a swimming pool and space for tents and caravans. There are non-naturist options too: the **Inn on the Shore** in Downderry has a super location (its name says it all) and offers recently refurbished ensuite rooms. Three miles along the coast at Portwrinkle, the **Beach House** has an outdoor sunken hot tub overlooking the shore.

And 13 miles to the west of Downderry, in and around Polperro, Fiona and Martin Nicolle have a range of **Classy Cottages**. Their development at **Lanlawren Farm** includes an indoor pool, and according to the brochure, 'We have only a few cottages so you will often enjoy the facility completely to yourselves. We leave your attire, while using the sauna, spa and pool, to your discretion.'

1. Vault Beach
2. Downderry

Granny's, Bodrugan and Edgcumbe
www.nationaltrustcottages.co.uk
Tel: 0870 4584422

Fort Cottage
www.gorran-haven.co.uk
www.ruralretreats.co.uk
Tel: 01386 701177

Seaview International Holiday Park
www.seaviewinternational.com
Tel: 01726 843425

Boswinger Youth Hostel
www.yha.org.uk
Tel: 01629 592708 / 0870 7706113

Carbeil Holiday Park (naturist)
Tel: 01503 250636

Inn on the Shore
www.coastandcountryinns.co.uk
ho@ccinns.com (head office)
Tel: 01503 250210

Beach House
www.beachhouse-cornwall.co.uk
Tel: 01460 30609

Classy Cottages
www.classycottages.co.uk
Tel: 01720 423000

Slapton Sands (pictured above, below and on the cover of this book) attracts hundreds of bare bathers at peak weekends, but has plenty of space for everyone

Although the cottages are definitely not naturist, this policy, which the Nicolles have operated for a number of years, is one of the most sensible we've seen. Another of their properties, **Foxes Lodge** (only 3 mins walk from Lanlawren and with access to the pool) has 'a sunny isolated garden, no neighbours – total privacy where you can hide away and worship the sun'. And from **Blanches** it's a 10-15 minute walk down to the shore and an almost unused private cove (map ref: SX177506).

Slapton Sands (Pilchard Cove)

Strete, near Dartmouth, Devon   *Map ref: SX838460*
A truly **idyllic and secluded** bare beach stretching more than half a mile which, on fine weekends, attracts hundreds of swimsuit-free visitors. The shore has plenty of space for everybody without feeling crowded and the views of Start Bay and the surrounding South Hams countryside are breathtaking. Rather than sand (as the name suggests) the beach consists of **fine shingle** which is comfortable to lie on, a bit hard going for walking and unsuitable for building castles! Nonetheless, it's popular with families, as well as couples and singles of all ages and the atmosphere is warm and friendly.

126

and interests as yourself.

Take the first step in changing your social life by filling in the coupon and we will send you, entirely without obligation:

FREE – a compatibility test, matching you with one of the many Dateline members who might like to meet you.

FREE – our full colour guide to how Dateline can work for you.

FREE – a copy of our book "All You Need Is Love", full of genuine stories of people whose lives have been transformed by joining Dateline.

Fax: 071 937 3146

Meet people from the hundreds of personal ads. in DATELINE MAGAZINE – available now at all good newsagents price £2.00.

Please send me in total confidence and without obligation:

♥ my compatibility test

♥ a full colour guide on how Dateline can work for me

♥ my copy of "All You Need is Love"
(Please enclose three first class stamps)

Start here

1. My sex is: Male ☐ Female ☐

My marital status is . . . .

My age is . . . .

My height is . . . .

I would like to meet people between the ages of . . . and . . . .

(Please write clearly in block capitals)

First Name . . . .

Surname . . . .

Postcode . . . .

Address . . . .

FREE

TEL:

out and bought about 18 heads! It was because the guy I'd been assisting had a bank of 16 big 1K lamps, each of which could be turned on individually to provide accurate fill-in. He'd shout to me "Turn number 14 on, lad."

Working with flash, Polaroid is essential to me. I use it for positioning and balancing of the lights, and even as an exposure check. You can initially balance flash heads by eye using the modelling lamps, but you have to fine-tune it by checking the results on film. By the way, Polaroids are rather like resin coated paper in the fact that you can't really over develop them; we tend to pull them after about 1¼ minutes. but if we left them for 2 minutes they would look the same.

Tungsten lights have to be positioned exactly. Two inches out either way can completely change the shot. You have to study your model's features: if she has slight bags under her

The people Harry Ormesher photographs in the studio are many and varied. They range from fashion models and Page Three girls to pop stars and celebrities. He explains how a consistent approach pays off:

Most of the lighting techniques I use are quite simple. They have to be because I'm photographing people all the time. Pop stars and celebrities are what the public want to see. They're not

much more important and there is a lot more movement in pictures thanks to high speed flash. If the clothes crease naturally with movement, it's okay. And now you light for the model as well as the garment.

As for the camera equipment, I simply choose the format that best suits the job. If it's a hat shot the result looks best in a square format so I use the Hasselblad. If it's an album cover then the same applies. The 6x7 is just right for magazine covers and a lot of editorial work.

I like 5x4 when I want to

www.vintagespankingmagazines.com

The sea is **extraordinarily clear**, if a little chilly, and the beach shelves steeply so children should be supervised. A windshield can be useful when it's breezy. Although nudity here is technically unofficial, few would realise, particularly as it's been a favoured naturist spot for more than 70 years. Pilchard Cove, at the far end of the beach, was the original nude area, but it's no longer necessary to walk that far. Access is relatively easy these days, being almost **entirely on the level**. There is a lovely hidden walled garden with picnic tables (not naturist) adjacent to the car park – a children's paradise, which is missed by many visitors. Toilets are nearby.

Travel south from Dartmouth on the A379 for 6.5 miles through the villages of **Stoke Fleming** and **Strete** (lots more stunning picture postcard views), continuing down the long hill to sea level. At this point do not follow the main road which turns sharply right along the top of the beach towards Torcross, but instead turn left into **Strete Gate** car park. In summer the pay and display parking, which has 101 spaces, fills early (10am at weekends, 11am on weekdays) and costs from 70p for 1 hour to £5 all day. Once it's full, alternative parking is difficult to find without a very long walk. From the car park entrance a few steps lead down to the shore. Turn left (north) along the path at the back of the beach and in a few hundred yards small fishing boats and winches mark the beginning of the clothes-optional area, which continues to Pilchard Cove at the end of the bay. Bus 93 from Dartmouth to Plymouth goes right past Strete Gate.

Naturist campers and caravanners are in luck. For years **Manor Farm**, in the village of Strete, has provided pitches specially for them. The spacious rustic site has a range of facilities and enjoys fine views over the bay. Perhaps the best thing is the relaxed and informal approach taken by owner Kate Gill, who has reserved a third of her 6-acre site for camping au naturel – if you haven't tried it, camping in the buff is nicer for practical reasons alone. On the other hand, for those seeking a romantic B&B with some serious luxury, **Hideaway** at Tamarisk Cove is on the outskirts of the village with direct access via steep steps to a traditionally clothes-optional cove. It enjoys super coastal views and there is a small, covered heated pool (skinny-dipping possible by arrangement with the owner), and has double rooms only. **Skerries** is a popular B&B in Strete with an English Tourism 4-diamond silver rating. The **Camping and Caravanning Club** site at Slapton is reasonably handy for the beach and the **Tower Inn** in Slapton has won many awards. The 3-star **Stoke Lodge Hotel** in Stoke Fleming has indoor and outdoor swimming pools as well as a sauna and Jacuzzi. More local accommodation and tourist info at: www.slapton.org, www.strete.org.uk and www.dartmouth.org.uk

1 Slapton Sands

Manor Farm Camping
www.manorfarmstrete.co.uk
Tel: 01548 511441

Hideaway
www.hideawaybb.co.uk
Tel: 01803 770549

Skerries
www.skerriesbandb.co.uk
jam.skerries@rya-online.net
Tel: 01803 770775

Camping and Caravanning Club
www.campingandcaravanningclub.co.uk
Tel: 02476 694995

Tower Inn
www.thetowerinn.com
towerinn@slapton.org
Tel: 01548 580216

Stoke Lodge Hotel
www.stokelodge.co.uk
mail@stokelodge.co.uk
Tel: 01803 770523

National Trust Properties
www.nationaltrustcottages.co.uk
cottages@nationaltrust.org.uk
Tel: 0870 4584422

Scabbacombe Sands

Between Brixham and Kingswear, Devon   *Map ref: SX919520*
This picturesque bare beach is less well known than others in
South Devon, but it is **highly recommended** by the locals.
Slightly off the beaten track, but not too difficult to get to and
fairly well used. The shore faces east and consists of a mixture
of sand and shingle. The cove is good for swimming and
provides sheltered lunchtime anchorage for visiting yachts from
nearby Dartmouth. Swimsuited and buff bathers happily share
the beach without any problems.

Travelling south-west from **Brixham** on the B3025 to
Kingswear and Dartmouth, take the left fork at **Hillhead**,
signposted Lower Ferry. Stay on the B3025 for a further mile
down Slappers Hill, then turn left into Broad Road (signposted
Coleton Fishacre). Continue across two small junctions then
turn left into **Scabbacombe Lane** at the T junction – there is a
National Trust car park on the right in three-quarters of a mile
(map ref: SX911522). A path leads down the hill to
Scabbacombe Sands and, although not difficult, the car park is
445 feet above sea level, so there is a longish haul back.
Naturists normally use the **left side** of the cove.

The **Chauffeur's Flat**, **Crockers Cottage**, **1 & 2 Coleton
Barton** and **Higher Brownstone Farmhouse** are all National
Trust holiday properties less than 2 miles from the beach.

Petitor

St Marychurch, Torquay, Devon   *Map ref: SX927664*
A local's beach, this one, but handy if you're in the area and want
to escape your swimsuit for a bit of all-over sunning and
swimming. It's a **steep descent** to get there which means non-
nudes are unlikely to stumble
on it by chance. Bare bathers,
on the other hand, have been
making the effort for more
than 25 years and it's a
popular spot on a sunny day.

It has so many regular
visitors, the beach has
developed a **community life**
of its own. The ever-useful
Nuff website www.nuff.org.uk
says there is a tendency for
single men to gather on the
left while women and family
groups head to the right. It's

Petitor beach has been enjoyed by
locals and tourists alike for 25 years.
Picture by Daniel Hoare

mainly pebbles but with some sand and large rocks for sitting in the sun. The clifftop views have attracted a few sad voyeurs in the past but they haven't managed to ruin naturist enjoyment of the place. There is a great website run by friends of the beach: http://friendsofpetitor.mysite.wanadoo-members.co.uk/

Drive or take a bus to **St Marychurch**, which is just outside Torquay on the B3199 to Shaldon. Park in **Petitor Road** or nearby, bearing in mind this is a residential area, and walk to the end of this road and down the long grassy slope. At the end turn left and follow the path down to the beach – it's a steep trek.

If you're looking to stay nearby, the **Albaston Hotel** on St Marychurch Road is an AA 2-star establishment not far from the beach. Further along the coast towards Torquay town centre, the **Downs Hotel** in Babbacombe Downs has fine sea views. Further info from: www.english-riviera.co.uk

Budleigh Salterton

Near Exmouth, Devon   *Map ref: SY060816*
A long wide open pebble shore backed by **dramatic sheer cliffs** of red sandstone. The bare beach here is officially recognised as 'clothing optional' – the local authority signs say

1 **Scabbacombe Sands**
2 **Petitor**
3 **Budleigh Salterton**

Albaston Hotel
01803 296758

Downs Hotel
www.downshotel.co.uk
01803 328543

Budleigh Salterton, below, has an offical bare beach that's easy to find and a great attraction if you're visiting the town

1 Weston Mouth

Handsard House Hotel
www.hansardhousehotel.co.uk
Tel: 01395 442773

Thatched Cottage Company
www.thethatchedcottagecompany.com
Tel: 01395 567676

Pooh Cottage Camp Site
Bear Lane, Budleigh, Devon EX9 7AQ
Tel: 01395 442354

The local council makes it easy to find
Budleigh Salterton's bare beach

so! Full marks to East Devon District Council. The pebbles are large so it's worth taking something comfortable to lie on and footwear suitable for swimming. Delightful scenery and good access from the town centre make it a popular spot at this pretty seaside resort. There are no facilities on the beach so take refreshments. When co-author Nick Mayhew-Smith was interviewed on **BBC Radio Devon** in 2004, a lady from the local Chamber of Commerce asked him to make sure Budleigh Salterton was included in *Bare Britain*. She said: "We want more visitors to use the naturist beach."

Budleigh Salterton is reached by the B3178 from **Exmouth**, or from the opposite direction using the A3052 and B3178 from **Sidmouth**. From the main street (Fore St) turn into Rolle Road, next to Hardings the clothes shop. At the end of the road, proceed down **Steamer Steps** on to the shore and turn right (west) for 500 yards to get to the naturist area. Toilets are located by the steps. There is very limited parking in nearby Cliff Terrace or you can park for up to 3 hours in Rolle Mews short stay in the town centre.

Handsard House Hotel in North View Road, Budleigh, mentions the naturist beach in its brochure. The local **Thatched Cottage Company** won the prestigious English Tourism Excellence 2004 Award and offers 5-star period properties to rent in the area. **Pooh Cottage** Camp Site is just over a mile from the beach and has a swimming pool and distant views of the sea.

Weston Mouth

East of Sidmouth, Devon   *Map ref: SY160878*
A lovely remote south-facing nude beach with that **away-from-it-all** feeling, which has gained many devoted enthusiasts over the years. It has pebbles and shingle, with some coarse sand at low

tide. Just over a mile from the nearest car park, it requires a longish climb down (and a longer one back) using a good footpath. The National Trust looks after most of the coast here. No facilities or shade so **go prepared**. A small number of clothed sunbathers and walkers enjoying the beach too do not cause any friction.

Take the A375 north from Sidmouth and turn left onto the A3052 at **Sidford**. After 2 miles turn right by the sign to the Donkey Sanctuary and the hamlet of **Weston**, where there is a small National Trust car park (there is additional parking at Higher Weston Farm). The footpath leads down through fields into Weston Combe and then there is a steeper descent to the shore. Most naturists turn right (west) on the beach and walk a short distance to the bare area. However, a few buff bathers choose to head to the left. There is an alternative path to the beach starting from **Dunscombe**.

Three handy places to stay are convenient for the beach: **Higher Weston Farm** offers B&B (4-diamond), **Leigh Farm** has 4-star self-catering in Weston and nearby **Dunscombe Manor** also provides self-catering accommodation. Less than a mile away, **Salcombe Regis** Camping and Caravan Park has mobile homes to rent.

Higher Weston Farm
www.devonfarms.net/sidmouth
Tel: 01395 513741

Leigh Farm
www.streets-ahead.com/leighfarm
leigh.farm@virgin.net
Tel: 01395 516065

Dunscombe Manor
www.dunscombe-manor.co.uk
dunscombe.manor@lineone.net
Tel: 01395 513654

Salcombe Regis Camping and Caravan Park
www.salcombe-regis.co.uk
Tel: 01395 514 303

Low tide at **Pednevounder** beach on Cornwall's south coast

South coast

Burton Bradstock

East of Bridport, Dorset　　　　　*Map ref: SY492886*
A beach of gently sloping coarse sand and shingle backed by
Jurassic clay cliffs which contain a variety of fossils. According
to **Dorset County Council** this is one of six beaches along its
coastline with an established tradition of naturist use. However,
it's less well known for bare bathing than other locations and is
generally quiet. Ramblers and walkers often use the shore in
preference to the coast path. Parts of the beach are covered at
high tide so check the times. Also, **strong currents** can make
swimming hazardous. There's an attractive café (clothed)
overlooking the sea, which serves cream teas and crab
sandwiches by the Hive car park.

Take the B3517 south east from Bridport to Burton
Bradstock, passing through the village centre in the direction
of **Abbotsbury**. In less than half a mile turn right into **Beach
Road**, signposted Hive Beach. The National Trust car park
and public toilets are close to the shore. Turn left (east) along
the sand and walk 800 yards to a quiet area away from
swimsuited bathers.

Lime Cottage in Burton Bradstock is 10 minutes' walk from
the sea and has details of the naturist beach on its website.
Pebble Beach Lodge B&B (4 diamonds) and self-catering is on
the coast road with good access to Hive Beach. **Vearse Farm** in
Bridport has three cottages, each with their own private indoor
swimming pool. **Freshwater Beach** Holiday Park is popular
with families and directly on the coast to the west of the village.
West Dorset Leisure Holidays have two mobile home sites at
Burton Bradstock. In the village, the 300-year old **Anchor Inn**
is renowned for its seafood. Local information is available at
www.burtonbradstock.org.uk

Cogden Beach

Swyre, near Abbotsbury, Dorset　　　　*Map ref: SY517872*
There are miles of **almost deserted** shoreline away from the car
parks at either end of this bare beach. The beach consists of
round pea-sized shingle heaped up by the sea – it's comfortable
to lie on but tiring for walking any distance. The top of the ridge
is colonised by sea cale and hides the seaward side of the beach
from the coastal path behind it. **Popular with fishermen** near
the access points but don't expect to see too many other people,
apart from possibly a handful of buff bathers. This is another

1 **Burton Bradstock**
2 **Cogden Beach**

Lime Cottage
http://mather.horstedkeynes.com
Tel: 01825 790306

Pebble Beach Lodge
www.burtonbradstock.org.uk (see
'Where to stay')
Tel: 01308 897428

Vearse Farm
www.vearse.co.uk
Tel: 01308 458434

Freshwater Beach Holiday Park
www.fbhp.co.uk
Tel: 01308 897317

West Dorset Leisure Holidays
www.wdlh.co.uk
Tel: 01308 422139

Two bare bathers enjoying the south
coast at Worbarrow Bay. Although
not an official naturist beach it is one
of many stretches of coastline where
you can find space to be yourself. For
listings of other remote places look
at www.nuff.org.uk or the thorough
naturist guidebooks produced by
Coast and Country (see page 199 for
details)

Coggs Cottage
www.dhcottages.co.uk/coggs.htm
Tel: 01929 553443

Guest West B&B
dorothyparkinson@btinternet.com
Tel: 01308 898381

The Manor Hotel
www.themanorhotel.com
Tel: 01308 897616 or 897785

The Old Coastguards
www.oldcoastguards.co.uk
Tel: 01305 871335

Litton Cheney Youth Hostel
reservations@yha.org.uk
Tel: 01629 592708 / 0870 7706113

Ringstead's impressive backdrop attracts many bare bathers, who gather at the eastern end shown in this picture by Rob Montier, of nude beach website www.sunaked.com

location identified by Dorset County Council as used by naturists. No shade or shelter. There is a small café and toilets at **West Bexington** car park.

Cogden is an extension of the shore at Burton Bradstock (see the previous entry) and is at the western end of **Chesil Beach**. There are three ways to approach the naturist section. From the National Trust car park 1 mile east of Burton Bradstock (off the B3157, map ref: SY503881) continue east along the coastal path between the back of the beach and **Burton Mere** for a mile. Cross over the shingle onto the foreshore for peaceful seclusion. The same area can be reached by walking west on the coast path from the car park at **West Bexington**. The third route is a former smugglers' path from **Swyre village**, which is just under a mile to the beach.

Coggs Cottage in West Bexington is 300 yards from the sea. Also in the village are the **Guest West** B&B and the exclusive **Manor Hotel**. The shore (swimsuited) is at the bottom of the garden of **The Old Coastguards** (4 cottages), a mile to the east of West Bexington. Three miles inland, **Litton Cheney** Youth Hostel provides self-catering accommodation. Refreshments are available at the Bull Inn at Swyre, tel: 01308 897250.

Ringstead Bay

Mid-way between Weymouth and Lulworth Cove, Dorset
Map ref: SY7638814

An **attractive beach** backed by high cliffs and with impressive views across to Weymouth. It consists of a mixture of pebbles and some sand when the tide recedes. The **swimming is good** and in fine weather the beach attracts a number of naturist visitors at the eastern end of the bay. It's a **suntrap** that gets very warm. Access to the nude section requires a walk along the pebble shore and so peace and quiet is generally assured. Sensible footwear is recommended. There is a café, toilets and a shop close to the car park in Ringstead.

From the A352 Dorchester to Wareham road turn south at the roundabout near **Warmwell** onto the A353 towards Weymouth. After just over 2 miles take a sharp left turn to **Upton** and **Ringstead**. A toll is charged for entering Ringstead village and using the car park, which is only 50 yards from the shore. Walk east along the beach for 20 minutes to the nude area at the far end of the bay. This is a naturist location mentioned by Dorset County Council.

Shore Cottage is at the eastern edge of Ringstead village and has its own rough path and steps directly to the shore. **Seafields** and **Aura Holworth** are two more holiday properties at Ringstead Bay (available through Dream Cottages). **Upton Farm Cottages** are a mile and a half from Ringstead and there is a large holiday park at nearby **Osmington Mills**.

Durdle Door (Bat's Head)

West Lulworth, Dorset   *Map ref: SY796803*

A super swimsuits optional beach on this outstanding World Heritage Coast, with high chalk cliffs providing shelter from the prevailing winds. Exceptional cases of **sunbathing in February** have been reported. The sand and shingle shore is very narrow at high tide and can occasionally be **cut off** under certain tide and wave conditions. Swimming is delightful when the weather's calm. It is close to the famous **Durdle Door** geological archway, one of Britain's most photographed beauty spots. Little Door, a miniature version of its big brother, is an interesting feature at the naturist end of the beach. Good footwear is advisable for the half-mile walk over pebbles to Bat's Head.

From the A352 Dorchester to Wareham road turn south onto the B3071 at Wool, signposted **Lulworth**. In the village of West Lulworth take the unclassified road west to Durdle Door Holiday Park, which is reached in 1 mile. Enter the site and park on the clifftop in the pay car park. There is a clearly marked

1 Ringstead Bay
2 Durdle Door

Shore Cottage (Property 317)
www.dorsetcoastalcottages.com
Tel: 01305 854454

Seafields & Aura Holworth
www.dream-cottages.co.uk
Tel: 01305 789000

Upton Farm Cottages
www.uptonfarm.co.uk
Tel: 01305 853970

Osmington Mills
http://osmington-mills-holidays.co.uk
Tel: 01305 832311

① Studland Beach

Durdle Door Holiday Park
Lulworth Estate
www.lulworth.com
Tel: 01929 400200

Gatton House
www.gattonhouse.co.uk
Tel: 01929 400252

Hambury Hotel
www.thehambury.co.uk
Tel: 01929 400358

> ❧ The National Trust
> **NATURISTS**
> **MAY BE SEEN**
> **BEYOND**
> **THIS POINT**

Studland, opposite and above, is said to be the closest Britain gets to a popular European naturist beach, with thousands of happy bare bathers visiting at peak weekends

path with steep steps leading down to Durdle Door – keep your camera at the ready. The route is safe but requires **reasonable fitness** for the climb back up! Don't be surprised to see hundreds of swimsuited visitors enjoying the beach below. Turn right and walk along the raised pebbles for just over half a mile for peace and seclusion. Naturists use the last 100-200 yards of shore before Bat's Head and Little Door. The location has been identified by Dorset County Council as used by naturists.

Caravans, motorhomes and tents are welcome at **Durdle Door Holiday Park** directly above the beach. Operated by Lulworth Estate, there are also holiday homes at the park and traditional cottages nearby. **Gatton House** B&B and the **Hambury Hotel** and health club provide accommodation in nearby Lulworth. The traditional thatched and beamed **Castle Inn**, set in prize-winning gardens at West Lulworth, offers tasty meals.

Studland Beach

Near Swanage, Dorset   *Map ref: SZ037846*
Probably the **best known** and **most popular** naturist beach in Britain, Studland is managed by the National Trust. Facing south-east, the beach consists of gently shelving fine pale sand, backed by dunes and an extensive nature reserve. The sea is generally calm and offers excellent swimming – in mid-summer the water even gets quite warm! **Refreshments are available** from a mobile kiosk, which the Trust parks in the centre of the nude area, and ice-creams are sold by a floating vendor who sails up and down the beach. No need to get dressed for either. The whole scene is bustling but easygoing and feels much more like **continental Europe**. With lots of families and people of all ages enjoying the shore this might not be the best choice for those seeking solitude at the height of the season.

The bare area is marked out by green-topped posts. It stretches for over 800 yards in length and for a short distance back into the dunes. **National Trust wardens** patrol reasonably unobtrusively on quadbikes and are on hand if assistance is required (tel: 01929 450259 or 01929 450500). There are occasionally reports of 'cruising' men and inappropriate behaviour in the dunes but don't let it put you off enjoying this place. Our advice is to **stay on the open beach** to avoid any distraction to your leisure and relaxation. On sunny weekends you are likely to be in the company of hundreds and sometimes thousands of like-minded sunseekers, basking naturally at this friendly naturist oasis. The National Trust has a visitor centre, restaurant, shop, toilets and showers at the huge Knoll Beach car park. **Wheelchairs** with balloon tyres for using on sand are available.

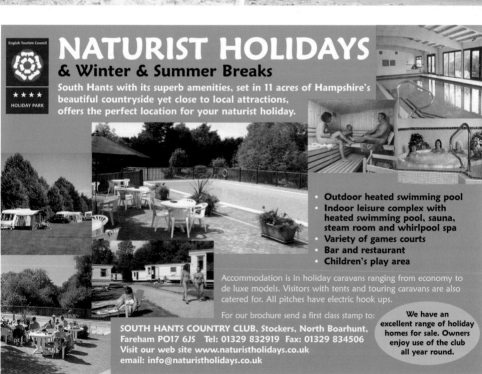

NATURIST HOLIDAYS
& Winter & Summer Breaks

South Hants with its superb amenities, set in 11 acres of Hampshire's beautiful countryside yet close to local attractions, offers the perfect location for your naturist holiday.

- **Outdoor heated swimming pool**
- **Indoor leisure complex with heated swimming pool, sauna, steam room and whirlpool spa**
- **Variety of games courts**
- **Bar and restaurant**
- **Children's play area**

Accommodation is in holiday caravans ranging from economy to de luxe models. Visitors with tents and touring caravans are also catered for. All pitches have electric hook ups.

For our brochure send a first class stamp to:

SOUTH HANTS COUNTRY CLUB, Stockers, North Boarhunt, Fareham PO17 6JS   Tel: 01329 832919 Fax: 01329 834506
Visit our web site www.naturistholidays.co.uk
email: info@naturistholidays.co.uk

We have an excellent range of holiday homes for sale. Owners enjoy use of the club all year round.

English Tourism Council
★ ★ ★ ★
HOLIDAY PARK

Rectory Cottage B&B
www.rectorycottage.co.uk
Tel: 01929 450311

Shell Bay Cottage B&B
Tel: 01929 450249

Bankes Arms Hotel
Tel: 01929 450225

Corner Cottage
www.faunscottage.co.uk
Tel: 01929 450309

2 Vine Cottage
www.cottagesdirect.com/doa059
Tel: 01929 480475

Sea Cottage
www.seacottagestudland.co.uk
Contact via website

Heath Cottage (Ref 213)
The Spot (Ref 203)
www.dorsetcoastalcottages.com
Tel: 01305 854454

Seaview and Currendon Cottages
www.nationaltrustcottages.co.uk
Tel: 0870 4584422

Knoll House Hotel
www.knollhouse.co.uk
Tel: 01929 450450

Studland is the biggest and some
would say best British bare beach

Studland is on the north-eastern tip of an area known as the **Isle of Purbeck**, separated from Bournemouth by the entrance to Poole Harbour. There is a vehicle ferry from **Sandbanks** on the other side of the harbour mouth, or the village can be approached from Wareham using the A351, turning onto the B3351 at **Corfe Castle**. It is also well signposted from the nearby resort of Swanage.

There are three popular routes to the naturist area. Our favourite is from the Knoll Beach car park; just walk down to the water's edge and it's then a pleasant 10-minute stroll along the firm sand. The bare area nearest the car park is particularly **family-friendly**. Perhaps one day the National Trust will extend the nudist section towards the Knoll end to accommodate the ever-growing number of discerning visitors. The second approach is to walk along the beach from the opposite direction. There is a National Trust car park near the ferry landing at the tip of **Shell Bay**. It is slightly further and likely to take 15-20 minutes at a brisk pace. The third route is to park on Ferry Road at Fire Point 6 – it's easy to find as there will be dozens of other vehicles parked in the vicinity. A footpath across the heath to the middle of the nudist area is just over half a mile long, but the soft sand can be heavy going in places.

Beware, it is not just the naturist area that's popular in summer, but the extensive dressed part of the beach as well. Consequently the roads can **quickly get grid-locked** as everybody tries to gain access to the car parks which, in spite of their capacity, fill up quickly. It is well worth arriving early to avoid the hassle. Dorset and Wilts Bus 150 from Bournemouth to Swanage will stop at any of the three places mentioned along Ferry Road. Some of the locals beat the rush and **sail to the beach** by boat from Poole Harbour.

There is a great choice of places to stay in the village of Studland and the immediate area. Bed and breakfast is available at **Rectory Cottage**, **Shell Bay Cottage** and the **Bankes Arms Hotel**. Meanwhile, **Corner Cottage**, **2 Vine Cottage**, **Sea Cottage**, **Heath Cottage**, **The Spot** and the National Trust's **Seaview** are available for self-catering. The family-friendly **Knoll House Hotel** offers the smartest and the closest

www.barebritain.com

accommodation to the naturist beach and the 2-star **Manor House Hotel** is nearby. Just outside the village **Currendon Cottages** (NT) are by the golf course and overlook the bay.

Lots more accommodation is available in Swanage and **The Quarterdeck**, a large modern house for rent, recommends the nude beach on its website. Slightly further afield near Wareham (9 miles), **Greenacre Naturist B&B** is popular, with attractive gardens for sunbathing naturally and a new spa pool.

There are plenty of places within a few miles for campers and caravanners. **Knitson Farm** is in a lovely rural setting and describes itself as 'minimum amenity'. In addition to the ordinary site there is a small informal naturist field, but no facilities apart from water and waste, so you must have your own toilet. **Burnbake Campsite** (only takes tents and motor caravans) occasionally has naturist weekends. A 4-star site with indoor swimming pool and caravans for hire, **Ulwell Cottage** Caravan Park is less than 3 miles from Studland, and **Swanage** Youth Hostel is also handy.

Studland info at: www.nationaltrust.org.uk; Swanage info: www.swanage.gov.uk; Purbeck info: www.purbeck.gov.uk. For more local naturist accommodation see the next beach entry – Hengistbury Head.

Hengistbury Head

Southbourne, between Bournemouth and Christchurch, Dorset
Map ref: SZ173905

Given how close it is to Bournemouth, Hengistbury Head is surprisingly quiet. It has been used by bare bathers for many years, though **not in huge numbers**, and it provides a different option for naturist seaside enjoyment. The Head itself is a magnificent rock outcrop, with prehistoric and Saxon settlements on its top. It has been declared a Site of Special Scientific Interest. The bare area is directly below the outcrop and consists of low, smoothed rocks above the high-tide level and fine shingle below. Currents and relatively heavy surf mean **caution is necessary** when bathing. The rocks make a good place to enjoy the sun and are above the occasional beach walkers passing by.

Head east from the centre of **Southbourne** to the car park at Hengistbury Head Visitor Centre, where there is a shop, café and toilets. In summer, Yellow Bus 12 or the seafront Land Train will get you there. Go down to the beach, turn left (east) and walk about 800 yards to the bare area.

There are lots of places to stay in Bournemouth and Christchurch. Tourist info: www.bournemouth.co.uk and

1 Hengistbury Head

Manor House Hotel
www.themanorhousehotel.com
Tel: 01929 450288

The Quarterdeck
www.purbeckholidays.co.uk
Tel: 01845 597614

Greenacre Naturist B&B
www.greenacrebb.fsnet.co.uk
Tel: 07831 116995

Knitson Farm Camping
www.knitsonfarm.co.uk
Tel: 01929 425121

Burnbake Campsite
www.burnbake.com
Tel: 01929 480570

Ulwell Cottage Caravan Park
www.ulwellcottagepark.co.uk
Tel: 01929 422823

Swanage Youth Hostel
www.yha.org.uk
reservations@yha.org.uk
Tel: 01629 592708 / 0870 7706113

www.christchurch.co.uk. Slightly further afield, near Wimbourne, **Dilly Dally's** offers naturist accommodation complete with swimming pool, 14-seater hot tub, sauna and steam room and not far away **St Annes** Naturist Caravan and Camping is at Three Legged Cross, near Ringwood.

There's more bare bathing (but no overnight accommodation) at **Rivendell**, a particularly impressive naturist club complete with swimming pool, sauna and Jacuzzi, whilst at **Bournemouth and District Outdoor Club** (BDOC) there are spaces for tents and touring caravans. Back in Bournemouth, **Hamilton Hall** at Boscombe is described as a 'private house retreat-style hotel' and periodically organises gay naturist weekends.

Taddiford Gap is an uncrowded naturist beach with views to the Isle of Wight and the Needles, visible in both pictures at the bottom. Picture below and bottom left by Charlie Simonds of naturist film producer Parafotos (www.parafotos.co.uk)

Taddiford Gap

Barton on Sea, Hampshire Map ref: SZ260923
Genuine naturists have been gathering at this spot in increasing numbers for a place to sit and read, sunbathe or swim undisturbed. It's a bit uncomfortable on the large pebbles without a mat but the **views are superb** towards The Needles and along the coast. The mud and shingle cliffs at the back are less attractive but the beach faces south so you'll have your back to them all day.

The bare bit lies on an undeveloped section of coastline between **Barton on Sea,** to the west, and **Milford on Sea**, to the east. Although never crowded with bare bathers, the shore here is clearly naturist and might have up to 20 or 30 bare souls on a sunny

weekend. Clothed beach users occupy the long stretches of coast on either side. Walkers sometimes pass through or behind the naturist bit but are usually polite enough not to bother people by gawping.

You can get to this beach from three different directions. In **Barton**, park in the pay and display car park and walk east along the cliff path for about half a mile. Cross a little footbridge and head down the gully to the sea. Turn left and you're on the bare beach. From **Milford**, it's about twice as far to walk, but easy enough to follow the coast path until you reach the naturist area.

Quickest of all is to use the pay and display car park on the B3058. The car park is on the seaward side of the road between Barton and Milford – bring plenty of coins if you're planning a long stay. From this car park, it's 5 minutes' walk along the path to the coast and the bare area starts 200 yards or so to the right (west). One final word of warning: traffic can be practically gridlocked through the New Forest on a summer weekend.

For local accommodation, especially naturist options, see the accommodation listing on this page for the previous entry, **Hengistbury Head**.

Calshot

Fawley, Hampshire   *Map ref: SU475006*
An attractive pebble beach far from the madding crowd where it's easy to find **peace and seclusion**. Backed by trees and other vegetation on higher ground belonging to a private estate; a sandy foreshore is revealed as the tide goes out. Swimming is good and there's always plenty of activity to watch as boats glide to and fro on the Solent.

The bare beach faces south-east and the Isle of Wight is less than 3 miles away across the water. Outside high summer this pretty strand loses the sun later in the day, so **get there early** to make the most of the rays.

Leave the M27 at junction 2 and travel south on the A326 towards **Hythe** and **Fawley**. Bear right at Fawley, taking the B3053 to Calshot, where there is a car park by the beach. Access the shore through a gap in the beach huts by the café and turn right (south-west), walking for 800 yards to the bare area which starts after passing the first of a series of dilapidated groynes. A large fence across the beach protecting a nature reserve marks the farthest end of the naturist beach.

Calshot is on the edge of the **beautiful countryside** of the New Forest national park, which has a good selection of holiday

1 Taddiford Gap
2 Calshot

Dilly Dally's (naturist)
www.naturistbreaks.co.uk
Tel: 01258 840908

St Annes Naturist Caravan and Camping (naturist)
Three Legged Cross
Dorset, BH21 6SD
stannescottage1@aol.com
Tel: 01202 825529

Rivendell (naturist)
www.rivendell-naturism.co.uk
Tel: 01202 824013

BDOC (naturist)
www.bdoc.co.uk
Tel: 01425 472121

Hamilton Hall (gay)
www.hamiltonhall.net
Tel: 01202 399227

Dale Farmhouse
www.dalefarmhouse.co.uk
Tel: 023 8084 9632

Old School House
www.newforestwheretostay.co.uk
Tel: 01590 612062

Langley Village Guest House
www.langley-hampshire.co.uk

Kingfisher Park
www.kingfisher-caravan-park.co.uk
Tel: 02392 502611

South Hants (naturist)
www.naturistholidays.co.uk
Tel: 01329 832919

Southsea Leisure Park
www.southsealeisurepark.com
Tel: 02392 735070

Bembell Court Hotel
www.bembell.co.uk
Tel: 02392 735915

Hamilton House
www.hamiltonhouse.co.uk
Tel: 02392 823502

cottages and bed and breakfasts. **Dale Farmhouse** B&B at Dibden and the **Old School House** at Beaulieu are reasonably handy. Even closer, just a few minutes' drive away is **Langley Village Guest House**. Three useful websites are: www.newforest.demon.co.uk; www.newforestcottages.co.uk; www.newforestbedbreakfast.co.uk

Browndown Point

Gosport, Hampshire   *Map ref: SZ578989*
This is a long almost level beach facing south-west with fine views across the Solent towards the Isle of Wight. There is a **tradition of bare bathing** here and with lots of space it has a pleasant 'away from it all' atmosphere. The pebble shore can make walking slightly tiring, but a number of visitors have remarked favourably on the enjoyment of their first-time naturist experiences at Browndown Point.

Nearby golfers and yacht crews sailing close to the shore are unconcerned about the lack of swimming costumes. Similarly, walkers following the coastal path along the shore remain unfazed. No facilities on the beach, but there are toilets by the car park and a **mobile snack wagon** in summer.

From junction 11 on the M27, take the A32 south towards **Gosport**. After approximately 4 miles turn right at the second of two roundabouts (which are close together), into **Military Road**, which is signposted HMS Sultan. Continue for 1.5 miles to the roundabout at the end of Military Road and cross straight over into **Gomer Lane**. After half a mile take the first exit on the next roundabout into **Stokes Bay Road** and after 100 yards the road sweeps sharply left as it reaches the coast. There is a car park by the bend.

Follow the fence down to the beach and turn right (north-west) along the shore. After 600 yards look out for the large 'concrete mushroom' structure, which marks the start of the naturist area. It is also possible to gain access coming the other way along the beach, from the Lee on Solent direction, but it is a slightly longer walk.

Less than half a mile from the parking area **Kingfisher Park** has mobile homes and space for touring caravans and tents. Fourteen miles and about 20 minutes away by car, **South Hants** Country Club and Holiday Centre for Naturists is a great place to stay. It has lovely indoor and outdoor swimming pools, spa pool, sauna and a range of leisure facilities, including high quality mobile homes for hire. There's also a licensed bar serving tasty meals and snacks. South Hants Club received a detailed and favourable review in the *Sunday Times* Travel supplement in 2004.

Eastney Beach

Portsmouth, Hampshire   *Map ref: SZ682990*
This beach might not be the most picturesque place in the world, backed as it is by a large **military radar station** surrounded by high security fencing, but it has two special attractions. First, it is officially recognised by **Portsmouth City Council** as a beach 'used by nudists' and second, it's quick and easy to get to – within a few yards of the car park and a local bus route.

The shore consists mainly of shingle and is good for sunbathing, but **take something soft** to lie on. Sandy patches, which appear as the tide goes down, are handy for swimming from. The beach attracts a cross-section of visitors, with a fairly high proportion of men during the week, but it's also popular with couples and families, particularly at weekends.

The beach is at the eastern end of the Portsmouth and Southsea seafront. Travel along the Esplanade and as it turns inland bear right into **Melville Road**. Continue to the T-junction with **Fort Cumberland Road**, where there is an adjacent car park. A path to the right of the entrance to the Defence Research Establishment leads to the beach. Turn left (east) and the bare area is within 100 yards.

Official nudist beach signs provided by the city council are usually in evidence, but unfortunately their periodic disappearance suggests they prove an **irresistible trophy** to some.

Almost next to the naturist beach and less than 5 minutes' walk, **Southsea Leisure Park** has mobile homes for hire and accommodates campers and caravanners, while the 3-diamond B&B **Bembell Court Hotel** and the 4-diamond **Hamilton House** in Southsea are both less than 2 miles away. The **South Hants** Country Club and Holiday Centre for Naturists at North Boarhunt, highlighted in the previous listing for Browndown Point, is about 25 minutes' drive.

1 **Browndown Point**
2 **Eastney Beach**

It won't win many awards as the most attractive naturist beach, but **Eastney** is a handy spot where you can bare and enjoy with the blessing of the local council. Picture by Charlie Simonds of Parafotos film makers (www.parafotos.co.uk)

THE BEACH BEYOND THIS POINT IS USED BY NUDISTS

Blackgang Beach

Near St Catherine's Point, Isle of Wight   *Map ref: SZ490756*

A lovely **south-facing naturist beach** which has long been enjoyed by locals and holidaymakers alike. The shore of fine shingle and tiny pebbles is comfortable for walking or lying on. It shelves fairly steeply into deep water and with strong tidal currents care is needed when swimming. With **breathtaking coastal views** and a sense of natural peace this secluded spot is the perfect place to spend the day. Access requires a bit of a scramble and there are no facilities nearby so take refreshments with you.

Although known as Blackgang Beach, it is at the point on the map marked **Rocken End**. From Niton village, near the southern tip of the island, turn into **St Catherine's Road** in the Undercliff (map ref: SZ505760) and then along the lane called Old Blackgang Road to a small car park. Take the footpath towards the sea, turning left (west) at the junction, which leads you over a previous landslip and eventually, after a steep climb, down to the beach. Alternatively travel west along the A3055 coast road to **Whale Chine**, walk down to the beach and then left (east) along the shore to the naturist area, a pleasant if strenuous 2 miles.

The south-facing **Blackgang Beach** on the Isle of Wight has long been an attraction for freedom-loving locals and tourists alike

Windcliff Manor Hotel in Sandrock Road is a 1-minute drive from the beach car park. **Bridge Cottage**, set in 2.5 acres of garden, is a quarter of a mile from the shore on the outskirts of Niton – available through Home from Home Holidays, which has five other properties to let in the village. In Brighstone, 15 minutes away by car, naturist B&B, a self-catering chalet, sauna and massage are available at **The Cottage**. Naturist camping is available at **Valerian Sun Club** near Havenstreet, less than 10 miles (30 minutes) from Blackgang Beach. Tourist info: www.islandbreaks.co.uk

Culver Beach

Sandown, Isle of Wight   *Map ref: SZ623853*
In contrast to Blackgang, our other recommended beach on the Isle of Wight, Culver, is **easy to access** and is not far from the seaside resort of Sandown on the southeast coast. Chalk cliffs rise above the shore, which is generally sandy with a shingle bank at the rear. The beach slopes gently and the water is clear so **swimming is normally excellent**. It's a popular spot with naturists and often gets busy in summer.

From Sandown, travel north-east along the seafront (B3395) following signs to the **zoo**, which is almost a mile out of town. There are a number of car parks in the vicinity, any of which are suitable. Walk onto the beach and **turn left** towards the white cliffs. It is then just a 10-minute stroll along the shore to the bare area beneath the cliffs.

Naturist camping is available at **Valerian Sun Club** near Havenstreet, less than eight miles (20 minutes) from Sandown. There are eight caravan sites in the Sandown area – details on www.islandbreaks.co.uk. The 3-star **Fort Holiday Park**, which has mobile homes for hire, is located not far from the seafront between the town centre and the zoo. The 5-star **Southland Camping Park** at Newchurch, which has won a string of awards, is ideal for motor caravans, tourers and tents.

Selsey Beach – West

Near Chichester, West Sussex   *Map ref: SZ826946*
Bare bathers have used the 2-mile stretch of West Beach between Selsey and Earnley at Bracklesham Bay for years – at least 40 in fact! The shore is **mainly shingle** at high tide, but as the water recedes acres of sand are revealed, interspersed with pebbles. A peaceful spot, which, even on the hottest days, may have **only a handful** of people relaxing au naturel on an otherwise deserted beach. Facing south-west, it can be exposed so a

1 **Blackgang Beach**
2 **Culver Beach**
3 **Selsey Beach – West**

Windcliff Manor Hotel
Tel: 01983 730215

Bridge Cottage (Ref: ES1609)
Home from Home Holidays
www.hfromh.co.uk
Tel: 01983 854340

The Cottage (naturist)
youneek@btinternet.com
Tel: 01983 740377

Valerian Sun Club (naturist)
www.valerian.fsworld.co.uk
Tel: 07931 281360

Fort Holiday Park
www.fortholidaypark.co.uk
Tel: 01983 402858

Southland Camping Park
www.southland.co.uk
Tel: 01983 865385

West Sands Caravan Park
www.bunnleisure.co.uk
Tel: 01243 606080

Vincent Lodge
www.vincentlodge.co.uk
Tel: 01243 602985

Selsey Country Club
www.selseycountryclub.co.uk
Tel: 01243 602165

Selsey beach – west has been enjoyed by bare bathers for more than 40 years. Picture by Rob

windbreak might be useful in breezy weather, although shelter can be found by the sea defence groynes. Overlooked from the top of the shingle bank, occasional mountain bikers and dog walkers are not concerned by nudists using this remote location, according to regular beach users.

From the A27 Chichester bypass take the B2145 signposted to **Selsey**. After 7 miles enter the town, ignore the turn to East Beach and continue through two sets of traffic lights. Take the right turn to **West Sands Caravan Park** and drive through the enormous park to the end of the road where there is free parking. Turn right (north-west) along the beach and the bare area begins after passing a few groynes and continues until approaching the developments at the other end of the beach.

West Sands Caravan Park has lots of accommodation and facilities, including a new multi-million pound pool and health suite complex, all close to the beach. In Selsey, 100 yards from the sea, **Vincent Lodge** luxury B&B has an English Tourism 4-diamond silver quality rating. Just outside town **Selsey Country Club** has one- and two-bedroom chalets for hire at the Golf Club. Tourist information and more places to stay: www.selsey.org.uk

Selsey Beach – East

Church Norton, near Chichester, W Sussex

Map ref: SZ878956

If you are in the area, or looking for a change of scene from Selsey West Beach (see above), you could check out this **attractive strand** near Pagham Harbour mouth. The area is popular with naturalists as well as naturists. No boats in the harbour, but instead a 1500-acre reserve which is home to wildfowl and waders – an **ornithologist's delight**. The seashore here has no passing traffic, making it ideal for sunbathing in the buff. As the tide goes out a few silt and mud patches are revealed in the sand and **strong river currents** flowing from the harbour can make swimming hazardous. Although never busy, the seclusion and privacy at Church Norton is attracting growing numbers of discerning clothes-free visitors each year – not surprising given the **stunning views** across the bay to Bognor and Littlehampton.

From the A27 Chichester bypass take the B2145 to Selsey. A mile before the town, where the road bends sharply right, turn left down the narrow lane to **Church Norton**. A small car park is situated at the far end of the lane. Walk down the track beside the Norman earthwork to the **Pagham Nature Reserve**. Continue along the edge of the harbour to the beach and turn left (north) along the shore and walk the 150 yards to the bare area, which then stretches for over a mile to the mouth of the river.

Norton Lea (3 diamonds) offers B&B in the hamlet of Norton, while **St Andrews Lodge Hotel** (4 diamonds) on the outskirts of Selsey has 10 ensuite rooms and a licensed bar. More accommodation: www.selsey.org.uk

1 Selsey beach – East
2 Shoreham

Norton Lea B&B
Tel: 01243 605454

St Andrews Lodge Hotel
www.standrewslodge.co.uk
Tel: 01243 607826

Shoreham

Portslade, Hove, East Sussex   *Map ref: TQ258046*

This bare beach has such an **unprepossessing approach** that first-time visitors suffer a heart-sinking feeling as they enter the industrial district of Shoreham Harbour to get to the nudist area. Surprisingly, although the beach is owned by the port authority and is within a stone's throw of all the commercial activity, the majority of users describe it as 'delightful'. This is probably because it is **screened from sight** and sound of the docks by a high retaining wall, making it relatively secluded and also sheltered from north winds.

The shore consists of banked pebbles, which get **sizzling hot** on fine summer days. A roll mat is recommended for lying on and windbreaks come in handy when there is a westerly or easterly breeze blowing. Sand is revealed at low tide and the swimming in calm weather is good, but avoid going near the mouth of the harbour. This is a **popular beach** for buff bathing and frequently attracts more than 100 naked souls at peak weekends. Although there are no facilities in the immediate vicinity, a short (clothed) stroll west reveals a bargain diner – a sort of beach bistro meets transport café. Many locals **prefer Shoreham** to the well-known and very public Brighton nude beach 3 miles along the coast.

From the centre of Brighton, travel west along the seafront, **Kingsway**, to Hove. Look for the windsurfing school at the lagoon (on your left) where the main road forks at traffic lights and veers inland. Proceed straight on at these lights towards the apparent **industrial dereliction** and turn left at the mini-roundabout. Grit your teeth and keep going as the road doglegs and snakes toward the dock area. A high concrete sea defence wall on the left marks the naturist area. A vertical **iron ladder** has been provided at a gap near the centre of the wall to facilitate access to the beach.

Alternatively, it's possible to **walk along the pebbles** from either end. There are 50 marked parking bays at the west end of the lorry park, but as usual the advice is get there early when it's busy, because they soon go. Don't be tempted to obstruct any of the commercial areas. Tourist info: www.visitbrighton.com, www.brighton.co.uk and http://tourism.brighton.co.uk

Brighton Black Rock Beach

Brighton, East Sussex   *Map ref: TQ327035*
Love it or loathe it, this is Britain's most accessible nudist beach – considered a **double-edged sword** by many naturists. On the positive side, it's well served by public transport and within walking distance of the centre of this famous Georgian seaside resort. Less endearing are the lack of seclusion and the sometimes **unseemly behaviour** of a minority of visitors. Pebbles and shingle, so typical of the region, make up most of the beach. It shelves steeply at the water's edge and getting in and out of the sea can be uncomfortable, but otherwise swimming is good. These days the beach attracts many gay users, with a predominantly male environment. Celebrations were held in 2004 to mark a **quarter of a century** of bare bathing at this official nude beach. Abundant facilities are available nearby.

Brighton can be reached with ease by all main means of transport. From the **Palace Pier** on the seafront, head east along Madeira Drive to Peter Pan's playground and cross the Volk's Railway on to the beach. City council signs indicate the nudist area. Limited parking is available behind the beach on **Madeira Drive**, with additional spaces within 300 yards.

Tourist information can be found at: www.visitbrighton.com, www.brighton.co.uk and http://tourism.brighton.co.uk/

Birling Gap

South of Eastdean, East Sussex   *Map ref: TV555965*
The **soaring white chalk cliffs** of the Seven Sisters form a dramatic backdrop to this secluded stretch of pebble shoreline.

A long history of naturist use means that any walkers who know the area are unlikely to blink at the sight of a bather enjoying the elements in their birthday suit.

On the other hand, **rocks falling from the cliff** are a real threat, so stay well clear of the fall zone. There are rocks and pebbles all along the shore – with the occasional patch of sand offering respite to feet and bottoms. There are also some terribly sharp rocks at the water's edge, which are exposed at low tide and well submerged at high tide. **Take great care** not to hurt yourself.

It's easy to find the beach. Take the A259 between Eastbourne and Seaford, and turn off south at the town of **East Dean**, following signs to **Birling Gap** and **Went Hill**. There's a pay car park at the hotel, and possibly some off-road parking for free. Take the wooden steps down to the pebbles and turn right (westwards). Walk about **500 yards** along the shore to the area where bathers traditionally start baring all. The further you walk, the more secluded the beach becomes. You might be the only one, but on a good day there are likely to be several others peacefully enjoying the beach their own way, and letting others do the same.

A café and toilets at Birling Gap are the nearest facilities, while the **Birling Gap Hotel** has a restaurant, café, bar and rooms.

1 **Brighton Black Rock**
2 **Birling Gap**

Birling Gap Hotel
www.birlinggaphotel.co.uk
Tel: 01323 423197

Birling Gap is a fine spot to get back to nature. Picture supplied by Shabden Leisure Circle

Fairlight Cove

Hastings, East Sussex   *Map ref: SZ680989*

History was made at Fairlight in 1978 when the local council designated it an **official naturist beach** – the UK's first. Of course plenty of beaches were used naked well before then, but the designation of this lovely remote cove paved the way for the more public launch of Brighton's naturist section the following year.

Fairlight has had a **mixed history** in recent years due to major problems with coastal erosion. The access route was closed by the local authority in 2002 after a wooden staircase was washed away from the cliff face, effectively making the beach **officially off limits**. But regulars still made their way down the unstable

Once a popular beach, **Fairlight** became much less frequented due to access problems but is still enjoyed by many determined bare visitors. Pictures all show Fairlight: bottom left by Robert Spatchurst; bottom right the beach at its busiest, before the steps were washed away, by Eric Holmes; below and opposite by Charlie Simonds of Parafotos (www.parafotos.co.uk)

cliff path and **dozens of bare bathers** still gather on a sunny weekend. The beach is included in our guide because the access situation may change, but users should note that as *Bare Britain* went to press the beach was no longer considered official by British Naturism and the access path was closed. For updates on the state of the path, visit the beach sections of either the NUFF website (www.armage.demon.co.uk/nuff) or British Naturism (www.british-naturism.org.uk).

The bay faces south and has **shingle with sand** at low tide. It lacks shade but the limestone cliffs and woodland backdrop are a **beautiful place to relax** as nature intended. Indeed, if your day at the beach looks threatened by poor weather you can console yourself with a walk in the lovely country park surrounding Fairlight Glen.

Bare bathers typically go to the east (left as you face the sea), but with the cliff path closed hardly any non-nude beachgoers make the effort to visit. It has been well used in the past and attracts a good mix of **groups and single visitors**. Be careful not to get cut off, particularly when exploring round the cliffs at the far eastern end of the naturist side, or walking in the direction of Hastings to the west.

From the A21/A28/A2100 junction in **Baldslow** (north of Hastings) take the B2083 signposted to Ore. After about 3 miles turn right at the A259 (it's a T-junction with traffic lights and a traffic island). Almost immediately, take a sharp left into **Fairlight Road**, signposted to the Country Park. After three-quarters of a mile there's a picnic site car park, from where it is a 1-mile walk to the beach. Cross the road and take the track downhill. Fork right before the short row of buildings, then left before you get to the field gate. The first bit of path through the woods is essentially a **stream bed**, very rough and often muddy. Keep going downhill until you come to a T-junction with a wide path. Turn left here and after a few yards you will cross a stream. The path to the beach is on the right but at the time of going to press was blocked with signs saying the beach access is closed.

Accommodation options nearby include the **Shear Barn Holiday Park** campsite beside the Hastings Country Park, and the **Chatsworth Hotel**, right on the seafront in Hastings with superb views over the Channel.

1 Fairlight Cove

Shear Barn Holiday Park
www.shearbarn.co.uk
Tel: 01424 423583

Chatsworth Hotel
www.chatsworthhotel.com
Tel: 01424 720188

① Leysdown

Connetts Farm Holiday Cottages
http://home.btconnect.com/
connetts-farm
Tel: 01795 880358

Shurland Dale
www.park-resorts.com
Tel: 01795 880353

Ashcroft Coast
www.park-resorts.com
Tel: 01795 880324

Shurland Hotel
www.hotels.uk.com/sheerness.htm
Tel: 01795 881100

Sheppey Guesthouse
www.sheppeyguesthouse.org.uk
Tel: 01795 665950

Leysdown Beach is relatively uncrowded but you may want a windbreak to protect yourself. Picture by Robert Spatchurst

Leysdown

Isle of Sheppey, Kent   *Map ref: TR051685*

A breezy sweep of coarse sand and fine shingle on the edge of the Medway estuary, Leysdown bare beach is undeveloped and **relatively uncrowded**. Backed by grassy sand dunes, the 250-yard long official nude area is well signposted at both ends by the Swale Nature Reserve. It's said to have a relaxed atmosphere and a band of friendly regulars.

There are good views of Whitstable and shipping in the Thames. Swimming is possible, but the foreshore becomes **increasingly muddy** as the tide goes out. Windbreaks are popular to shelter from the sometimes blustery conditions. Some users also use windbreaks for privacy, as a few selfish visitors have been known to stop and stare. There are no toilets or refreshments available at the beach.

Access to the **Isle of Sheppey** is by the A249 from the A2 or junction 5 of the M2 near Sittingbourne. Once over The Swale and on to the island, take the right turn after half a mile, on to the B2231 signposted to **Leysdown-on-Sea**. Don't be deterred by the air of a bygone era, with brash amusement arcades, sprawling caravan parks and ancient wooden beach chalets. Continue through the town, following the road along the beach for almost a mile to a Y-junction by **Muswell Manor** (site of the first powered flight in Britain in 1909), and turn left towards **Shell Ness**. The road progressively deteriorates into a track, passing more chalets and cottages, for almost another mile. Park directly behind the nude beach, which is reached after a 100-yard walk over the low-lying grassy sand dunes.

Connetts Farm Holiday Cottages (3- and 4-star) are 5 miles from the naturist beach, which is specifically mentioned on their website. Also nearby are two well-equipped holiday villages, **Shurland Dale** (4-star) and **Ashcroft Coast** (5-star), both part of the Park Resorts Group. The 3-star **Shurland Hotel** in the village of Eastchurch is particularly handy for Leysdown, or just outside Sheerness at Halfway Minster **Sheppey Guesthouse** offers B&B. Tourist information at: http://tourism.swale.gov.uk

50 films on DVD or video about naturism and naturist resorts...

...both in the UK...

...and overseas

**NEW RELEASE summer 2005:
Britain's Bare Beaches**

Send for our free colour brochure:
Parafotos Film Productions, PO Box 269, Pewsey,
Wiltshire SN9 6PD
Tel/fax: 01980 630761 Web: www.parafotos.co.uk

East coast

St Osyth

Clacton-on-Sea, Essex   *Map ref: TM115123*

Winter storms early in 2004 unfortunately washed away the approach road to this official naturist beach making access difficult, particularly at high tide. The nude area is close to the Colne branch of the Blackwater estuary and **caution is required** when bathing. The extensive south-facing shore consists of mainly sand and some shingle, with a few muddy patches appearing at low tide. A **nature reserve** at the far end of the beach is fenced off, while to the north lie remote marshes and dykes. The tranquillity is a world away from the bustle of nearby Clacton-on-Sea. St Osyth has long been a popular spot for nude relaxation, but **visitor numbers have reduced** since the recent storm damage.

From the outskirts of **Clacton** take the B1027 west, off the A133, towards St Osyth. Approaching the village take the left fork onto a minor road into St Osyth. In the centre, turn south on to **Beach Road** and continue to the sea wall at the end of the lane, which is by Hutleys Caravan Park. Refreshments are available at the Sailor Boy pub and there is also a café and shop. Walk west along the shore for 1 mile to get to the bare area.

Hutleys Caravan Park provides family accommodation with plenty of facilities. The naturist beach is mentioned on their website. The award-winning **Park Hall Cottages** offer luxurious self-catering close to the historic village of St Osyth. Nearby, 4-star B&B is available at **Pond House**, Earls Hall Farm, just outside Clacton. Further afield, at Sible Hedingham west of Colchester, **Pevors Farm Cottages** offer probably the highest standard of naturist accommodation in the UK (English Tourism Council 4 stars) including an indoor pool for skinny-dipping – more details on page 153.

Tourist info: www.essex-sunshine-coast.org.uk

Corton Beach

Two miles north of Lowestoft, Suffolk   *Map ref: TM547967*

Although not the prettiest stretch of Suffolk coastline, this beach has been given **official approval** for naturist use by the local authority. It's a reasonably popular stretch of pebbles, shingle and sand at low tide and is just 2 miles from Lowestoft. The beaches section of the local tourist website www.visit-lowestoft.co.uk lists the nude beach as one of the area's attractions, and there is plenty else to interest **holidaymakers** in the surrounding region.

1 St Osyth
2 Corton beach

Hutleys Caravan Park
www.parklandsleisure.co.uk/hutleys.htm
Tel: 01255 820712

Park Hall Cottages
www.parkhall-countrycottages.com
Tel: 01255 820922

Pond House B&B
www.earlshallfarm.info
Tel: 01255 820458

Pevors Farm Cottages (naturist)
www.pevorsfarm.co.uk
Tel: 01787 460830

Norfolk's **Holkham** beach, opposite, is one of the top naturist beaches in the UK and a highlight of the east coast. Picture by Mick Goody

Corton has official approval for naked bathing, and it's a much-appreciated attraction for bare-minded visitors to the region. Signs at either end indicate the naturist zone

The sloping shore makes access to the sea easy, and there is a row of groynes providing **shelter from the wind**. The beach is backed by a concrete breakwater protecting a steep grassy bank, with paths that run along above the bare area. A caravan park at the top overlooks the beach in places and is a handy place to stay if the beach is your main reason for visiting the area.

Corton has a good number of regular naturist visitors. At times a disproportionate number of men, often at the far end of the beach, has been noted – but a more mixed crowd gathers at popular times, particularly in the **first section** of the beach. It's an official naturist place so you have an absolute right to enjoy being naked here without anyone disturbing your day.

The beach is just south of the little village of **Corton**. Take the A12 from Lowestoft to Great Yarmouth and turn off for Corton down the **B1385**. The road ends in a T-junction, where you turn right. Drive into the **free car park**, marked by a sign saying 'Toilets' and 'Golf'. A concrete path from the north-east corner of the car park (left as you face towards the sea) leads across a road and down a **tree-lined gully** to the coast. Turn left and after 200 yards you'll see the signs indicating it's time to strip.

Many beach users stay at the clothed campsite **Azure Seas**, which is right by the beach. Two naturist holiday sites, the **Broadlands Sun Association** and **Merryhill Leisure**, cater directly for bare bathing tourists and are within 20-30 miles of Corton naturist beach.

Holkham Bay

Wells-next-the-Sea, Norfolk   *Map ref: TF876456*
Holkham has been voted **best British beach** for a bank holiday break by discerning readers of *The Times*, according to travel writer Chloë Bryan-Brown. We can't argue with that, and thankfully, because it is so vast – 3 miles long and up to half a mile wide – there is **space for everybody**. And don't worry, you won't find deckchairs and candyfloss here, just a beautifully unspoilt coastline and a big open sky.

Getting to the bare area requires a moderate but delightful walk along pretty tracks and paths, so it's never overcrowded, even at the height of summer. Backed by pine woods and surrounded by **Holkham national nature reserve** (the largest coastal reserve in England), this tranquil haven is the perfect place for relaxing naturally. Helpful signs provided by the Holkham Estate and English Nature identify the nude area on the western side of the bay. The landowners are supportive of naturist visitors, but request they **use the open beach** rather than the dunes, to avoid damaging the fragile plant communities.

The fine silky sand on this **family-friendly** beach is mixed with tiny shells and is ideal for building castles. The shore is almost flat so the sea goes out a long way, but youngsters (of all ages) will love paddling at the water's edge. However, care is needed as the **tide comes in quickly**. Set on the East Anglian coast, the weather is often bracing so it's well worth using a windbreak. English Nature describes it as somewhere to

1 Holkham Bay

Azure Seas Caravan Park
www.long-beach.co.uk/azure.htm
Tel: 01502 731403

Broadlands (naturist)
www.paston.co.uk/broadlands
Tel: 01508 492907

Merryhill Leisure (naturist)
www.merryhillleisure.co.uk
Tel: 01603 881411

Holkham's flat sands mean the tide comes in quickly. Picture Mick Goody

catch your breath in a busy world. Wardens and occasional local police patrols look after the naturists as well as the other visitors.

Even if you haven't been to the beach you might still have seen it – **Gwyneth Paltrow** got Holkham sand between her toes when the Oscar-winning *Shakespeare in Love* was filmed here. During the 19th century **Lord Nelson** spent many of his childhood days exploring this stretch of coast, and further back in history, the Vikings sailed up a creek through the salt marshes during the first millennium and built a fort at a place they called Holkham ('ship town' in Danish). There are no facilities so take your own refreshments and a picnic for a great day out.

Holkham is on the north Norfolk coast 2 miles west of **Wells-next-the-Sea** on the A149. In the village, opposite the entrance to Holkham Hall and by the Victoria Hotel, turn right (north) into **Lady Ann's Drive**, which heads towards the sea. There is a large car park on the left. From the car park continue on foot down the drive, turning left at the bottom, and follow the hardcore track keeping the Corsican pine woods on your right. Pass a small saltwater lagoon on your left and proceed half a mile to the **George Washington Hide**. Take the wooden

Holkham's huge expanse of sand, sea and sky has been used as a Viking settlement, a film set and of course a naturist beach. Pictures below by Charlie Simonds of Parafotos (www.parafotos.co.uk)

boardwalk which heads off from here and goes to the beach. At the shore turn left (west) to the signposted naturist area. The walk from the car park takes 20-30 minutes. Holkham is on National Cycle Route No 1 (more info from Sustrans: www.sustrans.org.uk) and is also served by the regular **Norfolk Coasthopper bus**.

The stylish and trendy **Victoria Hotel** in the village is part of the Holkham Estate and gets booked up well in advance during summer. The **Pinewoods Holiday Park** (4-star) between Holkham and Wells offers luxury lodges, mobile homes and fields for tents and caravans. In nearby Burnham-Overy-Staithe, **Flagstaff House** has quality self-catering next to the shore, and there are three National Trust holiday cottages in the village. In Wells the **Crown Hotel** has ensuite rooms and the food is highly recommended (*AA Pub Guide 2005*). A short distance inland from Wells, B&B with a Jacuzzi in the garden is available at **Meadow View Guest House**. Fifteen miles east along the coast, two of the properties at **Bolding Way Holiday Cottages** have sufficient privacy in their gardens to be of interest to discreet naturists, according to the owner. Holkham Hall, the classic 18th century palladian mansion in 3,000 acres of deer park is well worth visiting, especially if the weather misbehaves. Tourist info: www.holkham.co.uk

North Cotes Beach

Near Cleethorpes, Lincolnshire   *Map ref: TA379022*
A remote bare beach on the north Lincolnshire coast where the sea goes out for more than a mile revealing a huge expanse of sand flats. Traditionally used by naturists this **wild place** has no nearby development or facilities. It is easy to access by road, followed by a short walk from the car park. Great caution is needed to **avoid being cut off** when the incoming tide races across the flats – sadly there was a fatal accident a few years ago. However, it's perfectly safe for secluded sunbathing near the high-water section of the beach.

Travelling south from **Grimsby** and **Cleethorpes** on the A1031, in the direction of North Somercotes and Mablethorpe, go through the villages of **Humberston** and **Tetney**. After a further 3 miles you'll go past the turn to North Cotes village and after a quarter of a mile take the next turn left into **Sheep Marsh Lane**, signposted to **Horse Shoe Point**. Continue for 2 miles along the mainly dead-straight lane to the end, where there is a car park by the beach at Horse Shoe Point. At the back of the car park locate the sea wall (a grassy bank) and walk north-west along it for 700 yards in the direction of

1 North Cotes Beach

Victoria Hotel
www.victoriaatholkham.co.uk
Tel: 01328 711008

Pinewoods Holiday Park
www.pinewoods.co.uk
Tel: 01328 710439

Flagstaff House
www.flagstaff-holidays.co.uk
Tel: 01728 638637

National Trust Cottages
www.nationaltrustcottages.co.uk
Tel: 0870 4584422

Crown Hotel
www.thecrownhotelwells.co.uk
Tel: 01328 710209

Meadow View Guest House
www.meadow-view.net
Tel: 01328 821527

Bolding Way Holiday Cottages
www.boldingway.co.uk
Tel: 01263 588666

1 Easington Beach

Fleece Inn
Tel: 01472 388233

Crown & Anchor Inn
Tel: 01472 388291

Beech Farm Country Cottages
www.beechfarmcottages.co.uk
Tel: 01472 815935

Prospect Farm
www.prospectfarm.co.uk
Tel: 01472 826491

Marquis Of Granby
Tel: 01964 650108

Mountain Ash House
Tel: 01964 650742

Bluebell Cottage Kilnsea
www.theholidaycottages.co.uk
Tel: 01709 760044

Willows Caravan Park
www.highfield-caravans.co.uk/willows.htm
Tel: 01964 612233

The Ivy B&B
theivybandb@virgin.net
Tel: 01964 631586

Northcoates Point. Then take any one of the numerous paths down onto the shore for bare bathing bliss.

Guest accommodation is available at the **Fleece Inn**, in North Cotes, and also at the **Crown & Anchor Inn**, a riverside country pub at Tetney Lock. Just outside the village of Tetney, **Beech Farm Country Cottages** offer some of the nearest self-catering accommodation, while further east at Brigsley, **Prospect Farm** has a selection of 5-star cottages 15 minutes' drive from the beach.

Easington Beach

Near Spurn Point, East Riding of Yorkshire Map ref: TA394211
This is another isolated stretch of shore far from the madding crowd on the North Sea coast, where it's possible to have a whole sandy beach to yourself. You probably won't see many other bare bathers, but for a spot of **peaceful skinny-dipping** and sunning in the buff it takes some beating. It can be breezy, but low grass-topped clay cliffs give shelter from the westerly winds. Keen geographers should be aware the cliffs are being eroded by up to 6 feet a year as a result of a strong southerly 'longshore drift'. A prominent feature locally is the **large gas terminals** just down the road where 25 per cent of the country's natural gas comes ashore, but don't let that put you off. The beach feels miles from anywhere – and it is miles from anywhere!

Easington is actually 24 miles south-east of **Hull** and reached by taking the **A1033** out of the city as far as **Patrington**, then forking right on to the **B1445** to Easington. On entering the village turn left (north) into **Dimlington Road** at the T-junction, heading towards **Out Newton** and passing the gas terminals en route. After 1 mile the road meets the coast and then turns sharply inland. Scramble down onto the shore and go left (north-east) along the beach. Five to 10 minutes' walk should result in **complete seclusion** where you can be at one with nature. The beach to the south of Easington is also remote and worth exploring. A trip down to Spurn Head nature reserve on the spit that sticks out into the Humber estuary will reward you with amazing views and an **array of wildlife**, but no swimming.

The **Marquis Of Granby** pub in Easington has ensuite rooms and home cooking, and **Mountain Ash House** offers B&B in the centre of the village. Three miles south in the hamlet of Kilnsea **Bluebell Cottage** is available for self-catering. Up the coast at the small resort of Withernsea, the 4-star **Willows Caravan Park** has mobile homes for hire and spaces for tourers and campervans. At the inland village of Patrington, B&B is on offer at **The Ivy** (4 diamonds).

Druridge Bay

Amble, Northumberland   *Map ref: NZ273978*

A lovely spot with a clean sweep of golden sand backed by extensive dunes and an unpolluted, if slightly chilly, sea. The bay is long and wide stretching almost from **Amble** in the north to **Cresswell** in the south. The nude area is between the **Druridge Bay Country Park** and a mile-long section of the beach owned by the **National Trust**. It is popular with local bare bathers and has been used by naturists for over 50 years. The private owner of the shoreline used by nudists is understood to be **generally supportive**, provided they don't stray outside the recognised area. Occasional ramblers and dog walkers on the beach are unconcerned by visitors relaxing in the buff.

Druridge Bay is 24 miles north of **Newcastle upon Tyne**. Travelling up or down the A1068 main coast road, turn east onto the minor road at **Widdrington** towards Druridge. At the point where the road takes a sharp right turn (south) down the coast, turn left into the **National Trust car park** by the nature reserve and go as far north as possible. Walk on to the beach, turning left (north) along the shore and proceed past the end of National Trust section. The nude area starts a further 300 yards along and continues up to the point where **Chevington burn** crosses the beach.

Near the southern end of the bay **Cresswell Towers Park** has family holiday homes for hire and a range of leisure facilities. **Amblers Rest** in the village of Amble and **Sandy Knowes Cottage** at Low Hauxley, near Amble, are both self-catering properties. **Hagg Farmhouse** offers bed and breakfast and is on the A1068 2 miles south of Widdrington, while a little further inland **Northumberland Cottage** B&B (4 diamonds) is at Cheviot Moor.

Further tourist information is available online from either www.visitnorthumbria.com or www.northumberland.gov.uk/vg

Ross Back Sands

North of Bamburgh, Northumberland   *Map ref: NU148377*

Blissful seclusion, endless soft sands and **fabulous coastal views** make Ross Back Sands one of the nicest places in the UK for bathing as nature intended. It's not an official beach but there is enough space to allow **respectful bare bathing**, and you should expect other beach users to leave you in peace too. For even greater solitude the beach is backed by dunes and plenty of tall dune grass screens the sandy hollows.

The beach is particularly suited to bare bathing as this 4-mile stretch of sand has dead ends to both the north and south,

1 Druridge Bay
2 Ross Back Sands

Cresswell Towers Park
www.gbholidayparks.co.uk
Tel: 0870 442 9311

Amblers Rest
www.cottageguide.co.uk/amblersrest
Tel: 01665 714869

Sandy Knowes Cottage
www.northumbria-cottages.co.uk
Tel: 01665 830783

Hagg Farmhouse B&B
http://haggfarmhouse.co.uk
Tel: 01670 860514

Northumberland Cottage B&B
www.northumberland-cottage.co.uk
Tel: 01670 783339

Heading for a dip at **Ross Back Sands**

Ross Cottages
www.rosscottages.co.uk

meaning few walkers pass along the shore. Even on a sunny weekend there may be no more than a few dozen beach visitors, and the clothed ones tend to stay in the middle of the beach by the access path. Up to a dozen or so bare bathers use the north section of the beach, which ends in a **sandy peninsula** jutting towards Holy Island. The sea is clean and gently shelves into the cool North Sea waves. The one disadvantage of the beach's solitude is the **long walk** from the nearest parking. It's at least a mile from the little hamlet of Ross, through a gently undulating grass nature reserve.

Although Ross is not marked on some road maps, it's fairly easy to find. Heading north on the A1, about half a mile after passing the B1342 turning to **Bamburgh** look carefully for a right turn to **Ross**, down a minor road. This junction is just beyond the village of **Belford**. Follow the road and signs to Ross, where you can park just outside the village. Continue along the road by foot until it becomes a driveway and then a path leading through fields and grassy dunes to the sea. If you're heading south down the A1 from **Berwick-upon-Tweed**, pass through the village of Buckton and then turn left for **Elwick**. Follow the road and signs to Ross and follow the same directions.

Ross Cottages is a lovely collection of seven self-catering cottages at the very end of the road to the beach, which cuts the walk to about 20 minutes. The area is full of unmissable attractions, including Holy Island and Bamburgh castle, and has a good supply of tourist accommodation. More information from www.visitnorthumberland.com

Ross Back Sands has fabulous views across to Holy Island, and plenty of space to explore the shore without disturbing or being disturbed by other beach users

H&E naturist

The UK's leading naturist magazine read worldwide by everyone who enjoys a naked lifestyle

A monthly update of naturist news, views, reviews, where to go and what to do

H&E naturist magazine is full of nude fun naturally

Visit our website
www.henaturist.co.uk
e-mail newfreedom@btinternet.com
or call 01405 760298

North West

Haverigg

Millom, Cumbria   *Map ref: SD144780*

An enormous and lonely expanse of sand and dunes at the mouth of the River Duddon, adjacent to the **Lakeland Outdoor Naturist Club** (see page 171). Facing almost due south, this bare beach enjoys long sunny days when the weather's warm. However, the **neighbouring wind farm** suggests it's a breezy spot. Acres of shore are revealed as the tide recedes, but it can be dangerous to venture too far out on to the potentially treacherous flats.

Swimming is normally fine when the tide is high, but a longish wade-in may be required to achieve any depth. **Shelter and seclusion** are available in the dunes, but better still make arrangements to visit or stay at the club where there is plenty of space to relax naturally.

Haverigg is in south-west Cumbria almost 40 miles from the M6 motorway at junction 36. From the motorway take the **A590** to **Greenodd** (20 miles) and then the A5092 to **Grizebeck** (6 miles). From here it's back on to the A590, signposted to **Workington**, and after 8 miles fork left on to the A5093 for **Millom**. From Millom follow the local signs to Haverigg. There is a car park near the Inshore Rescue Boat station – walk west along the line of the dunes for just over a mile. However, if prior arrangements are made with the Lakeland Outdoor Club, it's possible to go to their site.

Lakeland Outdoor Club is a lovely naturist place to stay if you have your own touring caravan, motorhome or tent. There are no facilities apart from a tap so you need to be self-contained, but you are sure to be made welcome by the club members. If you prefer more facilities, including an indoor swimming pool, **Butterflowers Holiday Homes** in Haverigg offers static vans to rent and has 90 touring pitches with electric hook-ups. Also in Haverigg, **Quiet Cottage** provides self-catering and **BookCottages.com** has a further five holiday properties in the village. Nearby, on the outskirts of Millom, **Duddon Estuary Youth Hostel** is less than 3 miles from Haverigg. Local info: www.thisismillom.co.uk

Roanhead – Sandscale Haws

Dalton in Furness, Barrow, Cumbria   *Map ref: SD191757*

This is the first of two lovely bare beaches across the bay from Haverigg, on the southern shores of the River Duddon (the

1 Haverigg
2 Roanhead

Lakeland Outdoor Club (naturist)
(also see page 171)
www.loc.ic24.net
Tel: 01229 821738

Butterflowers Holiday Homes
www.butterflowers.net
Tel: 01229 772880

Quiet Cottage
www.cottagesdirect.com/quietcottage
Tel: 01229 772974

BookCottages.com
www.bookcottages.com

Duddon Estuary Youth Hostel
www.yha.org.uk
Tel: 01229 773937

Solitude and bare bathing often go hand in hand. Many nude bathers prefer remote locations rather than popular naturist beaches, and Cumbria's shore is a fine place to leave it all behind

Fairway Hotel
www.fairway-hotel.co.uk
Tel: 01229 461200

Chequers Hotel
www.chequers-hotel.co.uk
Tel: 01229 462124

Abbey House Hotel
www.abbeyhousehotel.com
Tel: 01229 838282

Orchard Cottage
www.orchardcottageulverston.co.uk
Tel: 01229 463591

Stable Cottage
www.southlakescottages.co.uk
Tel: 01229 826969

second is the following entry, on Walney Island). Less than 4 miles from the heavy industry of **Barrow in Furness**, this is a haven of peace and tranquillity. Designated a national nature reserve by English Nature and managed by the National Trust, it has a mosaic of sand dunes including dune stacks. Salt marsh, shingle and freshwater marsh are also part of the reserve and several nationally scarce plants are found here. **Swimming is not recommended** because of the strong currents and deep river gullies, but there is plenty of seclusion, making it an ideal spot for catching some sun in the buff.

Travelling south on the **A595** from **Grizebeck** towards **Dalton in Furness**, turn right onto the **A590** at the roundabout outside Dalton, in the direction of Barrow in Furness. At the next roundabout (2 miles away) continue on the A590, but immediately after the roundabout turn right into **Oak Lea Road**, which runs north into **Hawthwaite Lane**. At the end of the lane there is a car park and toilets by the beach at Roanhead. Walk half a mile west to the dunes for clothes-free relaxation.

The brand new **Fairway Hotel** (opened September 2004) is conveniently located in Hawthwaite Lane, at the opposite end from the beach, while the **Chequers Hotel** has ensuite rooms in the centre of Dalton. The **Abbey House Hotel**, set in 14 acres of gardens, is next to the ruins of the famous Cistercian Furness Abbey founded in 1127. **Orchard Cottage** has cosy accommodation for two and **Stable Cottage** offers self-catering on a working farm, on the outskirts of Barrow.

Local info: www.dalton-in-furness.org.uk

Walney Island – North End Haws

Barrow in Furness, Cumbria   *Map ref: SD174734*
The second remote bare beach on the southern side of the River Duddon is on Walney Island (the first is at Roanhead, listed above). Backed by dunes of **fine soft white sand** reaching 60 feet high, this area of the island is a national nature reserve managed by English Nature and the Cumbria Trust for Nature Conservation.

It's well off the beaten track and enjoyed **mainly by naturists**, but don't expect a crowd – just a few locals and holidaymakers 'in the know'. Occasional clothed walkers and naturalists exploring the reserve are unlikely to cause any problems to bare bathers also enjoying the solitude. Swimming can be dangerous due to strong currents and deep gullies. **Hollows in the dunes** provide delightful suntraps and there are fine views over the estuary to the hills in the Lake District. A wonderful place to spend a summer's day. There are no facilities so remember to take refreshments with you.

From Barrow in Furness take the **A590** over the **Jubilee Bridge** on to the **Isle of Walney**. Head across the island to **North Walney** and the seafront at **Earnse Point**. A track heads due north parallel to the beach, past the airfield, until it terminates at the sand dunes. It's a 20-30 minute walk through the dunes, or along the shore if the tide is out, to reach the bare area at **North End Haws**. All the way along to the tip of the island is generally accepted as clothing-optional. For plane-spotting in the buff, the Walney Airshow takes place in the summer and the aircraft fly directly over the beach.

Local info: www.walneyisle.co.uk, which includes aerial photos of the beach).

The **King Alfred Hotel** and the **Brow Head Hotel** both offer B&B in Vickerstown, on Walney. For camping, caravanning and mobile homes **Walney Island Caravan Park** is at South End. Over the bridge in Barrow, the **Victoria Park Hotel** is in the centre of town close to the shops.

Additional accommodation: www.barrow.visitor-centre.co.uk

① Walney Island

King Alfred Hotel
www.thekingalfred.co.uk
Tel: 01229 474717

Brow Head Hotel
www.browheadhotel.activehotels.com

Walney Island Caravan Park
www.walney-island-caravan-park.co.uk
Tel: 01229 472823

Victoria Park Hotel
www.victoriaparkhotel.co.uk
Tel: 01229 821159

Scotland

The west coast of Scotland is one of the most beautiful places in the world, yet seldom visited. This makes it easy to find a patch of deserted sand and sea, but it also means that popular tourist activities such as nude bathing have not developed. With the sole exception of Cleat's Shore, on the Isle of Arran, the beaches listed in this section are **not naturist** and should only be regarded as bare beaches in the sense that they may be devoid of other visitors. If you do decide to enjoy a spot of unofficial skinny-dipping, do so with care and respect for others. If in doubt, cover up rather than risk offending: it's not only the midges here who can make life uncomfortable for bare bathers!

Gemini Cruises
Crinan, Lochgilphead, Argyll
Tel: 01546 830208
Tel: 07765 813950

Farsain Cruises
Craobh Haven, Argyll
Tel: 01852 500664

Island of Jura

All Jura sites can be accessed by charter boat (which will drop you off and collect later) from Gemini Cruises or Farsain Cruises.

Glengarrisdale Bay, North Jura   Map ref: NR647971
This bright sandy beach is near a red-roofed mountain bothy or

Corpach Bay, on Jura, pictured left, is a stunning location that seldom sees visitors. Much the same can be said of parts of the Scottish countryside, as this picture taken overlooking Loch Turret shows. Picture by Stuart Forbes

hut where it is possible to stay, or to camp outside next to the sea. Interesting caves, wild deer, birds, goats and an **abundance of wild flowers** add to the attractions of this remote and unspoilt spot. Access the beach by boat or by path across the hills from the east side of Jura.

Bagh Uamh nan Giall Bay   *Map ref: NR663985*
In the north of Jura and near the famous whirlpool of **Corryvreckan**, this small beach is well sheltered in most winds, unspoilt and seldom visited. Access is by boat.

Corpach Bay   *Map ref: NR561910*
One of the most **stunning localities** on the west coast of Scotland yet seldom visited. Looks out to **Iona, Colonsay and Oronsay**. Massive cliffs and huge sand hills create a sheltered place for baring all, and fresh water makes camping a possibility. The beach is hardly ever visited except by wild deer, goats and many seabirds. Fantastic wild flowers adorn the shore. Access is by boat.

Shian Bay   *Map ref: NR530877*
Another absolutely stunning beach, this time a long flat bay facing south-west with wide open vistas to Colonsay and Oransay with dunes, fresh water and places to camp. Seldom visited and natural attractions include deer, wild goats, birds and flowers. Access is by boat or by foot across the hills from West Loch Tarbert. **Interesting caves for exploring** add to the adventure.

Glen Batrick Bay   *Map ref: NR517802*
On the southern side of Loch Tarbert this wide open, unspoilt shore has **long stretches of fine sand** with interesting caves to explore and fresh water available. The usual wild animals and flowers await nature lovers. Access is by boat or across the hill from the public road.

Morvern Peninsula

This remote area of the Highlands is accessible via ferry from either Corran or Oban, to the south of Fort William, or by road from Fort William. Despite its beauty few people visit the area and once again **discreet bare bathers** have been known to enjoy the solitude without problems.

Loch Arienas – beach one   *Map ref: NM694506*
This quiet, unspoilt beach lies by the side of the freshwater loch

and river mouth. Access is from the A884 about half a mile away. The beach is surrounded by **fine trees**.

Loch Arienas – beach two   *Map ref: NM677511*
This small beach is also on the loch's shore and close to a public road, overlooked by **hills and woods**.

Moidart, Lochaber, Highlands

Glenaladale, Loch Shiel   *Map ref: NM822739*
This small, south-facing beach at the mouth of a river is surrounded by high hills and **mountain scenery**, backed by trees on the side of a long freshwater loch. It is very remote and seldom visited. Access by path from Glenfinnan, or by hire boat or canoe from Dalilea House near Acharacle, on the southern end of the loch. Tel: 01967 431253.

Sandy Point, also on Loch Shiel at map ref: NM781709, is a similar spot.

Samalaman Bay   *Map ref: NM663777*
Near Glenuig, by the public road between Acharacle and Lochailort, this **secluded and sheltered bay** has views out to the Atlantic and the islands of Eigg, Muck and Rum.

Ardnamurchan, Lochaber, Highlands

Gortenfern, near Kentra Bay, Acharacle   *Map ref: NM613690*
Several secluded bays here are **backed by dunes** with wide open views south-west towards the Atlantic ocean. Secluded and remote, they are accessible by private road from Kentra near the foot of Loch Shiel.

Sanna Bay   *Map ref: NM440696*
Near Ardnamurchan Point – which is the most westerly point on the British mainland – there are numerous quiet corners which are largely unvisited. Sand dunes and **beautiful views** to the Inner Hebrides add to the attraction of this south-west facing bay.

Arisaig and Morar, Lochaber, Highlands

Glasnacardoch Bay   *Map ref: NM705804*
On the **remote and wild** Ardnish Peninsula, accessible only by track (2-hour walk) from the Mallaig to Fort William road, this is a remote and uninhabited coastal stretch. There is a small south-facing beach, known locally as the 'Singing sands' because it makes a noise when you walk over it.

Lagg Inn
www.arran.net/lagg/inn
Tel: 01770 870255

Shannochie and Kilbride Cottages
www.shannochiearran.demon.co.uk
Tel: 01770 820291

Brodick Tourist Information
The Pier, Brodick, Isle of Arran,
KA27 8AU
Tel: 01770 302401

Cleat's Shore

Lagg, Isle of Arran, Ayrshire   *Map ref: NR944209*

Surprisingly, this away-from-it-all bare beach enjoys **official recognition** for its nude bathing status. Located near the southern tip of the beautiful Isle of Arran, it consists of fine sand interspersed with rock and shingle. Palm trees outside the nearby pub attest to the favourable effect of the Gulf stream hereabouts; the sea bathing on the west coast of Scotland is warmer than you might expect in the summer.

The views across Kilbrannon Sound to Kintyre are delightful. Look out for **seals** basking just offshore. Don't expect to find lots of other visitors, dressed or undressed, at this remote haven. You may well have the beach to yourself, so just soak up the **peace and solitude**, assured in the knowledge you are on a fully designated naturist beach.

The ferry from **Ardrossan** on the mainland takes just under an hour to reach **Brodick** on the east coast of Arran. The modern roll-on-roll-off ferry makes the crossing five times a day. Take the **A841** south then west for 18 miles to **Lagg**. It takes about 30 minutes if you drive yourself or 45 minutes on the local bus. Continue through Lagg and soon after the village a sign to 'Cleat's Shore mile' points to a lane on the left. It's possible to drive down the gated track almost to the shore and park close to the buildings by the naturist section.

In addition to visiting the quietest official naturist beach in Britain, and quite possibly the entire world, the island itself is well worth visiting in its own right. Arran is often described as '**Scotland in miniature**', with its wonderful blend of wild scenery, pastoral views, mountains and unspoilt coastline. Even if the weather is no good for the beach you won't be stuck for **places to visit**.

The **Lagg Inn** is the handiest place to stay, just a short distance from the naturist beach. It has a choice of ensuite accommodation, wholesome meals and can provide visitors with ferry-inclusive packages. **Shannochie and Kilbride Cottages** offer quality self-catering overlooking the sea in the nearby village of Shannochie, less than 2 miles from Lagg. More cottages on the island can be found at the website: www.cottageguide.co.uk/arran

A range of accommodation is also available from the **Brodick Tourist Information Office**.

Also see the two local websites: www.arran.net and www.visitarran.net for more information, including transport timetables and fares.

Corpach, on Jura (opposite) is as beautiful as it is remote, backed by cliffs and sand hills that lend seclusion to a skinny-dipping visitor

Wales

Malltraeth Bay

Newborough Warren, Anglesey   *Map ref: SH388640*

This big wide open sandy beach is perfect for communing with nature. Stretching for over a mile in length, Malltraeth Bay has all the **undisturbed space** anybody could wish for. The backdrop of dunes and an extensive Corsican pine forest add to the sense of natural beauty. Used unofficially by naturists for years, it takes a moderate walk to get to the bare area. When you arrive you might find you have the whole place to yourself. The beach is exposed to **westerly breezes** blowing off the Irish Sea, but shelter can be found at the edge of the dunes. Take care not to damage the fragile plant communities. Swimming is good so it's a lovely spot for some skinny dipping. There are no facilities nearby. Toilets are available at the Forestry Commission car park.

Follow the **A55** North Wales coast road to **Anglesey**, cross the Menai Strait by the Britannia bridge then take the **A4080** to the village of **Newborough** – a good place to stock up with provisions at the local store before entering the forest. The

1 Malltraeth Bay

Come rain or shine, **Morfa Dyffryn** beach in Wales, pictured opposite, is a much loved asset to nude bathers. Picture opposite top by Charlie Simonds of Parafotos (www.parafotos.co.uk), below by Steve Thompson.
Malltraeth Bay on Anglesey, below, has far fewer visitors but is just as spectacular in its own way. Picture by Karen Thorley of the excellent nude beach website www.sunaked.com

Awelfryn Caravan Park
www.awelfryn.co.uk
Tel: 01248 440230

White Lodge Caravan & Camping
www.whitelodgecaravanpark.
freeservers.com
Tel: 01248 440254

Feisdon Bach and Swn y Môr
www.anglesey-cottages.co.uk
Tel: 01407 840479

Garnedd Ddu Holiday Cottages
www.garneddholidaycottages.co.uk
Tel: 01248 714261

Nant-Yr-Odyn Hotel
www.nantyrodyn.co.uk
Tel: 01248 723354

Getting to **Morfa Dyffryn** naturally;
picture supplied by Ron Bell

Warren is signposted from the village and is approached along **Church Street**. There is a charge for access and parking. Walk onto the beach and turn right (west) in the direction of **Llanddwyn Island**, which is just over a mile away. Follow the line of the forest until the island is reached. Cross the narrow isthmus into Malltraeth Bay and a further 350 yards along the shore the world should have been left far behind. This is the area favoured for going au naturel.

However, some local naturists recommend alternative seclusion, by turning left rather than right at the beach access from the car park, in **Llanddwyn Bay**. It's a brisk 25-minute walk (south-east) along the shore to a point where the beach curves slightly inland adjacent to high sand dunes, which provide sufficient privacy for baring all (map ref: SH426619). The busier areas will be more or less out of sight. There is room to relax by the edge of the dunes but don't go into them as it is a **protected nature reserve**. The water here is relatively sheltered, and gets warm as the tide goes out, leaving shallow pools for wallowing in. **Views of Snowdonia** are superb – especially on summer evenings. Be discreet if using this area.

Awelfryn Caravan Park and **White Lodge** Caravan and

Camping Park are both right on the edge of the forest in Newborough and cater for touring caravans, motorhomes and tents. Two self-catering properties, **Feisdon Bach** (at Malltraeth) and slightly further up the coast **Swn y Môr** (at Llanfaelog), are available from Anglesey Cottages. **Garnedd Ddu Holiday Cottages** are 2 miles from the Britannia bridge at Llanfairpwllgwyngyll. For more luxurious serviced accommodation, the **Nant-Yr-Odyn Hotel** near Llangefni is 7 miles from Newborough. For more accommodation choices see: www.menaiholidays.co.uk, www.nwhc.co.uk and www.walestouristsonline.co.uk/anglesey

1 Morfa Dyffryn

Morfa Dyffryn

Between Harlech and Barmouth, Gwynedd   Map ref: SH557242
This is the **jewel in the crown** of Welsh bare beaches and one of Britain's favourites. With an inspiring location in the Snowdonia National Park it attracts a dedicated following of naturists from across the country and even visitors from overseas. Although Morfa Dyffryn has been a popular spot for stripping-off since the 1930s, **Gwynedd Council** took the welcome decision five years ago to make **bare bathing official**

Hundreds of bare bathers seek out the space of **Morfa Dyffryn** to be themselves. Picture from Barry Allen

and designated more than 1,000 yards of coastline for enjoying in the buff.

During hot summer weekends hundreds of holidaymakers enjoy the beach as nature intended. The golden expanse of sand shelves gently into the sea, providing perfect conditions for swimming. The water quality passed the **highest standards for bathing** in 2004. The naturist area is a 15-20 minute walk along the shore from the car park and is particularly popular with families, ticking all the right boxes for a fine day out at the seaside. Flying kites, building castles, collecting shells, catching fish, watching birds, spotting dolphins, playing beach games, paddling at the water's edge – and not forgetting some well-deserved relaxation – all are on the agenda here. There are no facilities so **take your own refreshments**, and a windbreak might come in handy. A variety of **wildlife** including rabbits, stoats, foxes, polecats and badgers live in the extensive dunes behind the shore, which form part of a national nature reserve. Tantalising views across the bay to the Lleyn Peninsular and glimpses of **distant mountain peaks** inland simply enhance the serenity of the beach.

The **A496** coast road between **Barmouth** and **Harlech** passes within a mile and a half of the beach. Between the villages

Most regulars take a windbreak to **Morfa Dyffryn**; apart from the sea breeze there's little else to take the edge off this perfect bare bathing haven. Picture by Charlie Simonds of Parafotos (www.parafotos.co.uk)

of **Talybont** and **Dyffryn Ardudwy** turn seawards into **Fford Benar Lane**, signposted Traeth (Welsh for beach). A small chapel at the junction is a useful landmark. The narrow lane leads to a car park close to the beach and there are toilets nearby. A boardwalk has been constructed through the dunes on to the shore and a helpful display board provides directions for the naturists. Turn right (north) and after a moderate stroll along the sand signs announce the start of the nudist area. It's possible to get closer by paying for parking at the **Dyffryn Seaside Estate**. A third option is to approach the beach from the opposite direction, walking a slightly longer distance, south from **Shell Island**. The beach enjoys surprisingly good **access by rail**. The Welsh Coast line from Barmouth to Porthmadog runs just inland, and the Dyffryn Ardudwy stop is less than 2 miles' walk from the bare area.

There is a good choice of local holiday accommodation. **Benar Beach Camping** includes a secluded naturist area for tents and tourers. **Dyffryn Seaside Estate** has a pub, restaurant, fish and chip shop and an indoor swimming pool. The estate has bungalows and mobile homes for hire and they also accept tents, campervans and touring caravans. For those looking for a simpler experience without any facilities, informal camping is available at **Glyn's Field** (tents only). Bed and breakfast is available at **The Old Farmhouse** (with a swimming pool) and **Pentre Mawr Farmhouse** in Dyffryn Ardudwy, while on the hillside overlooking the coast, a mile outside the village, **Byrdir Farm House and Studio Cottages** offer B&B and self-catering. Back in the village, deluxe self-catering is available at **Ystumgwern Hall Farm**. A little over a mile to the north of the naturist shoreline, **Shell Island** claims to have the largest camping area in the UK, with over 300 acres to choose from (tents only). There are also holiday flats and chalets and a small harbour for launching dinghies. **Llanbedr Youth Hostel** is near Shell Island and the 2-star **Ty Mawr Hotel** is in the same village. Luxury B&B is available at **Erw**, a contemporary Wolsey Lodge, five minutes up the road at Llanfair. For a very special treat, **Maes-y-Neuadd**, voted Welsh country house hotel of the year in 2003 and with a 2-rosette restaurant, is just 10 miles north of Morfa Dyffryn.

It's good to see North Wales Tourism promoting Wales's first official naturist beach on their website: www.nwt.co.uk. Information about the Snowdonia National Park can be found at www.eryri-npa.co.uk, while if you're coming here as a tourist, dramatic Harlech Castle is a must-see for holidaymakers in the area: www.secretsnowdonia.co.uk/harlechcastle.htm. More local accommodation: www.wales-holidays.co.uk

Benar Beach Camping
Tel: 01341 247571 / 247001

Dyffryn Seaside Estate
www.dyffryn-seaside-estate.co.uk
Tel: 01341 247220

Glyn's Field
First field on right on road to Dyffryn Seaside Estate – no booking, turn up and pitch – tents only

The Old Farmhouse
www.ukworld.net/oldfarmhouse
Tel: 01341 242711

Pentre Mawr Farmhouse
www.pentre-mawr.co.uk
Tel: 01341 247413

Byrdir Farm House, Studio Cottages
www.byrdir.co.uk
Tel: 01341 247200

Ystumgwern Hall Farm
www.ystumgwern.co.uk
Tel: 01341 247249

Shell Island
www.shellisland.co.uk
Tel: 01341 241453

Llanbedr Youth Hostel
www.yha.org.uk
Tel: 01629 592708 / 0870 7706113

Ty Mawr Hotel
www.tymawrhotel.org.uk
Tel: 01341 241440

Erw
www.erwharlech.co.uk
Tel: 01766 780780

Maes-y-Neuadd
www.neuadd.com
Tel: 01766 780200

Whiteford Burrows

Gower Peninsular, West Glamorgan   Map ref: SS443955

Almost 50 years ago, in 1956, the Gower was the very first place in Britain to be officially declared an **Area of Outstanding Natural Beauty** and it's not difficult to see why. On the northern edge of the peninsula, at Whiteford Burrows, there are more than 2 miles of unspoilt and secluded sandy shore backed by a national nature reserve with an array of fauna and flora. Owned by the National Trust and leased to the Countryside Council for Wales, this stunning bay has **surprisingly few visitors**.

It's a reasonable walk to get to the more remote parts of the beach traditionally enjoyed by discreet naturists. Even in midsummer much of this lovely strand is deserted, particularly towards Whiteford Point. Just beyond the point the **disused Victorian lighthouse**, constructed of ornate cast iron, makes a fascinating landmark. Strong currents in the bay, close to the mouth of the River Loughor, mean bare bathers should **exercise extreme caution**. It's hard to believe this peaceful haven is less than 15 miles from the city centre of Swansea; it feels a world away. The sand is soft and yellow and there are plenty of hidden

The Gower's **Whiteford Burrows** has surprisingly few visitors, but naturists make use of the solitude for discreet bare bathing. Picture by Roy Wilmot

hollows at the edge of the dunes to find your own perfect spot for basking in the buff.

Leave the **M4 motorway** at junction 47 taking the **A483** south for 1.5 miles to the junction with the **A484**. Turn right here (second exit on the roundabout, signposted to **Llanelli**). After 2 miles turn left onto the **B4296** for a few hundred yards, then right onto the **B4295** to Llanrhidian. Continue on unclassified roads following the signs to **Llanmadoc**. There is a car park by the church in the village. Walk down the gated track through **Cwm Ivy** and enter the National Trust property, following the path to the beach. Turn right on the shore and head north for 20 minutes at a brisk pace (or slightly longer at a gentle pace) to find complete seclusion. The further you go the more deserted it gets. An alternative easy path strikes off to the right by the pine trees at the back of the dunes, soon after arrival at the National Trust boundary. This is a slightly shorter route on a well marked track through the reserve to the remote part of the beach. As there is no clearly defined naturist area **use common sense and discretion** in the unlikely event other clothed people are in the vicinity.

If you would like to stay in the nature reserve close to the beach **Burrows Cottage** is a former forester's home available from the National Trust. Higher up the track towards Llanmadoc, **Cwm Ivy Court Farm** also has holiday cottages to let. In and around the village **Tallizmand Guest House** and **Forge Cottage** offer bed and breakfast and the **Farmers Arms**, a former public house, has been converted into two self-catering properties. **Barn Studios** are part of an art centre offering residential painting courses. **Whiteford Bay Leisure Park** has static caravans for hire.

Local info: www.llanmadocgower.co.uk

Traeth Mawr

Monknash, Vale of Glamorgan   *Map ref: SS900709*

A **rugged and dramatic** bare beach backed by towering cliffs rising vertically over 200 feet above the shore. Traeth Mawr ('big beach') is on the Bristol Channel, noted for having the second largest tidal range in the world. Skinny-dippers should be aware of **dangerously strong currents** in the estuary. Local naturists are regular visitors and rate this picturesque spot highly. In addition to peace and tranquillity, it is said to have a friendly atmosphere and is untroubled by occasional clothed beach users. Designated a site of special scientific interest because of its **unusual geology** – the cliffs consist of alternate layers of limestone and shale which are clearly visible – the bay is flanked by large flat rocks, so smooth and symmetrical they look like a

1 Whiteford Burrows
2 Traeth Mawr

Burrows Cottage
www.nationaltrustcottages.co.uk
Tel: 0870 4584422

Cwm Ivy Court Farm
www.welshwelcome.co.uk
Tel: 01792 386388

Tallizmand Guest House
http://tallizmand.co.uk
Tel: 01792 386373

Forge Cottage
www.forgecottagegower.co.uk
Tel: 01792 386302

Farmers Arms
www.thefarmersarms.co.uk
Tel: 01792 390997

Barn Studios
www.barnstudios.co.uk
Tel: 01792 386678

Whiteford Bay Leisure Park
Tel: 01792 386676 / 01792 386242

Bwthyn y Castellis
www.quaintholidaycottages.co.uk
Tel: 01446 796471

Oast House
www.theoasthouse.net
Tel: 01446 792240

Curriers Guest House
www.smoothhound.co.uk/hotels/
curriers.html
Tel: 01446 793506

West House Country Hotel
www.westhouse-hotel.co.uk
Tel: 01446 792406

Acorn Camping and Caravanning
www.campingandcaravansites.co.uk
Tel: 01446 794024

Crossways House
www.crosswayshouse.co.uk
Tel: 01446 773171

Fontygary Leisure Park
www.fontygaryparks.co.uk
Tel: 01446 719464 / 710386

Traeth Mawr's superb setting is worth a trip in its own right – with the added attraction of a skinny-dip. Picture below by Roy Wilmot, and opposite showing the flat rocks looking like a man-made pavement by Charlie Simonds (www.parafotos.co.uk)

giant **man-made pavement**. Large expanses of sand are revealed on this south-west facing shore as the tide recedes and the cliffs provide welcome shelter from cool northerly winds. The beach is approached by a pleasant 15-20 minute amble down a steep wooded valley alongside a gurgling stream. Note that parts of Traeth Mawr can be cut off at high tide: check before you go at www.bbc.co.uk/weather/coast/tides

Travel west from **Cardiff** on the **A48** towards **Cowbridge**, but avoid the town centre by using the bypass. Just before the end of the bypass take the slip road signposted **B4270 Llantwit Major**. From Llantwit Major take the unclassified road south-west to **St Donats**, **Marcross** and **Monknash**. Turn left in the centre of Monknash down the narrow lane to **Cwm Nash**. The road soon passes the Plough and Harrow public house and in less than a mile from the village there is a large car park in a field. The footpath down Cwm Nash to the beach is clearly marked. Turn right on the shore and the bare area is reached in a further 800 yards.

Bwthyn y Castellis, described as a quaint holiday cottage, offers the option of a 'holistic holiday' in Llantwit Major. Also in the historic town, B&B is available at the **Oast House**, **Curriers Guest House** and the **West House Country Hotel**. Just outside town, **Acorn** Camping and Caravanning has static caravans for hire as well as space for tents and tourers. **Crossways House** in Cowbridge offers B&B and has a self-catering flat. Twelve miles to the east, at Rhoose near Cardiff Wales Airport, **Fontygary Leisure Park** has mobile homes on the cliff top and a leisure centre with a gym, indoor pool, sauna, Jacuzzi and steam room. Local information available from: www.llantwitmajorvale.co.uk

Republic of Ireland

Corballis

Donabate beach, near Swords, Co Dublin
An attractive long sandy beach backed by grassy dunes, with a feeling of space and seclusion. Facing east towards the Irish Sea with views of Lambay Island in the distance, it catches the **early morning sun** perfectly. Nude bathing is enjoyed at the lower southern end of the strand just in front of the dunes. In warm weather this fine unofficial bare beach attracts a number of enthusiastic but discreet naturists.

Occasional clothed walkers appear unconcerned by those who prefer to take their leisure in the nip. It's less than 30 minutes from **Dublin** and is particularly handy for the airport. There is a choice of no less than six top-class golf courses in the immediate vicinity and a notable landmark nearby is the **Martello Tower** No 6, which was built in 1830 after the Napoleonic wars.

Corballis is situated a short distance from the main Dublin to Belfast road. Travel north from Dublin, past the international airport, to the town of **Swords**. Continue over a series of roundabouts and after another mile a sign signals a right turn off the dual carriageway to **Donabate**. Follow the road through Donabate village and directly to the beach, where it's possible to drive on to the shore. Turn right (south) and proceed as far as possible, but **beware of soft sand**. Continue on foot in the same direction for 15-20 minutes to find the secluded bare area. There is a station in Donabate on the Dublin to Belfast railway line.

1 Corballis
2 Vico Road

Irish Naturist Association
These pages were compiled with the help of the Irish Naturist Association
www.esatclear.ie/~irishnaturist/

Corballis beach, below, is used by discreet bare bathers; picture from the Irish Naturist Association. Pictured opposite by Andrew Winfer, a bare bather tests the warmer waters of the Mediterranean

Vico Road

Outside Dalkey village, near Dun Laoghaire, Co Dublin
This is a small clothing-optional bathing place reached by descending a steep but safe path. There is **generally good tolerance** between skinny dippers and swimsuited users, but discretion is advised. Bare bathing is most popular in the **early morning**, before the costumed visitors arrive. The

1 **Brittas Bay**

2 **Curracloe**

Vico Road has a tradition of bare bathing early in the morning, and at all times skinny-dippers use the place with consideration for clothed swimmers; picture supplied by the Irish Naturist Association (www.esatclear.ie/~irishnaturist/)

sea is reached via a series of steps which are accessible at all states of the tide and there's also a small pool which provides shelter from the waves and swell. A hard-to-reach **rocky cove** to the right of the swimming area provides a useful retreat for enjoying the sun au naturel, if it gets too busy later in the day. Caution – the path to the cove has been eroded and is very narrow, so **extreme care** is required. This location is not suitable for children or the elderly and infirm.

From the village of **Dalkey**, to the south of **Dun Laoghaire**, take the **Sorrento Road** and then turn right on to the coast road (**Vico Road**). The bathing place is signposted. Walk across the footbridge and follow the path. To the left is the way down to the changing huts and diving board.

Brittas Bay

Near Mizen Head, Co Wicklow

Favoured by campers and caravanners, the main beach at Brittas Bay gets particularly busy with holidaymakers from Dublin in mid-summer. Perhaps it's because this stunning bay is reputed to be the finest on the whole of the east coast. Almost 2 miles south along the shore is where discerning bare

bathers relax in the buff. Though technically still unofficial, it is said to attract more au naturel users than anywhere else in Ireland. With **beautiful views** this secluded area is ideal for swimming, sunbathing or a naked stroll along the beach to soak up the ambiance. No facilities so take a picnic, refreshments and plenty of sun cream. There is lots of **soft white sand**, but with a stony strip to cross between the dunes and the sea it's advisable to wear sandals. Also, be alert to the possibility of **offshore currents**. The beach is nonetheless highly recommended for all-over tanning.

Brittas Bay is popular with ordinary bathers but has space at the southern end where discerning visitors enjoy the elements in their birthday suits; picture supplied by the Irish Naturist Association (www.esatclear.ie/~irishnaturist/)

Travel south from Dublin towards **Wexford** on the **N11** and 9 miles beyond **Rathnew** turn left at **Jack White's Cross**. There is a pub (Jack White's) on the corner. Proceed down the road to the T-junction and turn right, following the coast for just under 2 miles. Look out for a group of fir trees and gateposts marked 'Buckroney' at the next road junction. Park and walk through the gate beside the sign for **Buckroney Sand Dunes**, following the path to the beach. At the shore turn left and walk north until fencing is visible up on the dunes – the traditionally bare area stretches from here to the stream further along the beach.

Curracloe

North of Wexford town, Co Wexford
This scenic blue flag beach stretches for miles and is particularly safe for bathing. Naturists use the **completely undeveloped** southern end of the shore which is backed by woodland and offers peace and tranquillity – you might even have the area to yourself. The **fine yellow sand** is pleasantly comfortable for lying on. Discretion is required at weekends as there are often more clothed visitors. The other end of the beach, to the north of Curracloe village, famously featured in the opening sequences of **Steven Spielberg's** Oscar-winning World War II drama, *Saving Private Ryan*.

From **Wexford** access is via the **R741/742** road, or from **Enniscorthy** take the **R744** road to **Blackwater** and then go south on the **L304**. The coastline in this area is one long beach. Keep to the right at the junction in **Curracloe** and right again at the next junction to reach the car park beside the wood. Walk down to the sand dunes and along the edge of the wood for 10-15 minutes to reach the traditionally bare area of the beach.

Inch Strand

Between Anascaul and Castlemaine, Dingle Peninsula, Co Kerry
The south-west coast of the country is renowned for its world-class beaches and Inch Strand will not disappoint – rated as **one of the best**. Getting fine sunny weather here might need just a touch more Irish luck than on the east coast, but it's a gamble well worth taking. The Gulf stream certainly helps and it's hard to think of anywhere better to enjoy being at one with nature.

The 2-mile long beach is on the southern side of the famous **Dingle peninsula** and is backed by extensive dunes. It is part of a sandy bar that almost reaches across to Glenbeigh on the Iveragh Peninsula, to form Castlemaine's superb natural harbour. In summer the entrance to the beach is usually well populated with costume-wearing visitors, but a brisk 15-minute walk along the shore brings seclusion and open space for baring all. **Sea otters, seals and dolphins** are often seen in the area and Inch Strand is yet another iconic film location, this time chosen by David Lean for shooting *Ryan's Daughter*. Naturists from across Europe have known and used this unofficial spot for years. We hope that one day the Irish Tourist Board will feel able to guide bare beach lovers here.

Travel 7 miles south from **Tralee**, the capital town of County Kerry, on the **N70 to Castlemaine**. Turn right on to the **R561** coast road and Inch is reached after 12 miles. The main entrance to the blue flag beach is signposted and has parking available. Walk south down the beach for half a mile away from the crowded area to discover a back-to-nature nirvana.

Yellow Strand

Near Drumcliff Bay, Co Sligo
This is a beach right off the beaten track and probably best suited to escapists. As the name suggests, it's a fine long strand of yellow sand located on the north side of **Sligo Bay**. A haven for occasional naturist holidaymakers and locals, but don't be surprised if the only company is your own. Completely unspoilt and undeveloped, this remote shore has been proposed as an official National Heritage Area (NHA). Vehicular access is something of a challenge, which reduces the

number of visitors. It is not too far from Trawalua bare beach (next listing), so well worth exploring if you are staying in the area and **feeling adventurous**.

Travel north from Sligo on the **N15** in the direction of **Donegal**. Proceed through **Rathcormack** and continue to **Drumcliff**, turning left off the main road (signposted **Carney**) shortly after passing through the centre of the village. Go though Carney and turn sharply left at the end of the village. Continue over the next crossroads (with a pub on the left), then take the next turn to the left (sign for **Ballyconnell**). Disregard all roads left and right for 1 mile, go straight over the next crossroads, and after 0.3 miles take the next lane to the left. The lane goes all the way to the beach. However, it's essential to **use the parking area** on the right hand side of the lane and walk the last 500 yards to the end. The landowner will be a virtual prisoner if beach users obstruct the lane.

1 Inch Strand
2 Yellow Strand
3 Trawalua Beach

Trawalua Beach

Cliffoney, Co Sligo
This delightful sandy beach forms a **broad golden arc** backed by extensive dunes. It's located a short distance up the coast

Trawalua's arc of golden sand attracts a friendly crowd of local bare beach users at the northern end. Picture by Declan Glynn

from Yellow Strand (previous listing). Open to the full force of the Atlantic swell, so dramatic waves crash on the shore in stormy weather. The northern end of the beach, near a rocky outcrop, is the favoured spot for baring all.

A band of **sociable locals** provide a warm welcome to like-minded visiting beachbums – just say hello. This is a well known, if unofficial, location in Irish naturist circles and is described as family-friendly. There are stunning views of Benbulben and Benwiskin in the distance, through the dunes.

Strong sea currents mean that swimming is not recommended, and there are warning signs to that effect. A nearby German-owned equestrian centre means horse riding on the shore is popular, but does not cause the swimsuit-free folk any difficulty. Lookout for 'Sligo Bare' an amiable regular committed to keeping the beach free of flotsam and jetsam that's washed up. He suggests it would be a great place for someone on their first bare beach day out: easy access, a beautiful setting, great people and largely undisturbed – what more could you ask for! Sligo Bare also has a useful website with more details of the bare beaches in Sligo: www.geocities.com/sligobare

The village of **Cliffoney** is situated on the main **N15 Sligo to Donegal road**, north of Grange and south of Bundoran (Co Donegal). In the village, turn on to the road to **Mullaghmore** for just 300 yards. Park opposite the gates at the bottom of the hill. Walk through the gates, past the football pitch, across the stream, and keep beside the water course down to the shore. Turn right and go 250 yards north to reach the bare area near the end of the beach.

Trawalua, below, has fabulous views but strong currents make the sea dangerous. Picture by Declan Glynn. For bare bathing in the Atlantic, pictured opposite, there are hundreds of other places in western Europe; picture by Charlie Simonds (www.parafotos.co.uk)

Best of British

At their best, UK naturist places combine the peace and beauty of the British countryside with the cheerful ambience of European naturist resorts. Here are our choices of the best places to bare all

1. Studland, Dorset

This popular, sandy National Trust area is the most popular of the UK's naturist beaches and a fine location for holiday makers. Details on page 38

2. Morfa Dyffryn, Gwynedd

A huge stretch of sand with space to be yourself, Morfa Dyffryn was the first official bare beach in Wales and is enjoyed by locals and tourists alike. Pic by Steve Thompson. Details on page 79

3. Slapton, Devon

This much-loved favourite has a great countryside setting, comfortable fine shingle and hundreds of freedom-loving bathers at the busiest times of the year. Details on page 28

4. Holkham, Norfolk

The endless sands of Holkham's gently shelving shore are backed by pine forest. Up to half a mile of golden sand is exposed at high tide. Pic by Mick Goody. Details on page 59

5. Pednevounder, Cornwall

Tricky access but stunning cliff top scenery make this one of the most photogenic of all UK bare beaches, with an easy mix of bare and clothed bathers side by side. Details on page 25

1. Pevors Farm, Essex

This modern, four-star luxury development is newly opened and offers a different type of naturist holiday to the traditional club venue. Details on page 153

2. South Hants, Hampshire

A classic British naturist club, rated by the Sunday Times for it's great holiday atmosphere and friendly mix of members and visitors. Details on page 138

3. Southleigh Manor, Cornwall

This perfect holiday location is much loved by visitors from both the UK and overseas, handy for sight-seeing in the county. Pic by Charlie Simonds. Details on page 124

4. Broadlands, Norfolk

Voted British Naturism club of the year in 2004, Broadlands enjoys both a natural woodland setting and plenty of leisure facilities. Pic by Steve Thompson. Details on page 147

5. Tything Barn, Pembrokeshire

The unique coastal setting allows visitors to indulge in some bare seawater bathing, a rare treat among UK naturist clubs and resorts. Pic by Roy Wilmot. Details on page 181

Boat for nude snorkelling and beach visits. Body Painting and Party Nights

Eagle Peak Spain Naturist Complex
www.eaglepeakspain.com

4WD nude mountain safaris for nude hiking and swimming in fresh- water pools

Singles welcome

High quailty self-catering apartments with sun terraces. Over-looking a naturist beach with 5 others nearby. Club -house with Spa bath, TV with satellite and video Boules Court, Large Roof Sun Terrace, Tropical Orchard Garden. Friendly atmosphere.

Bare holidays

Many bare beach fans first discovered the joys of naked bathing on holiday abroad. Some of the finest European beaches have dressed and undressed sunbathers sitting next to each other without a care in the world. It's the easiest place to find out why so many choose to bare.

Booking a bare-friendly holiday has never been easier, with plenty of UK travel agents geared to take you to the destination of your dreams. And even closer to home, why not consider staying at a UK naturist club or resort? British bare holiday options are listed on page 116.

This section summarises some of the beautiful places listed in Bare Beaches, the companion guide to Bare Britain. We highlight the big five bare beach destinations of France, Spain, Greece, Croatia and Portugal – but it's possible to discover bare beaches, lakes and rivers in nearly every European country.

For the intrepid traveller, exotic beaches in the Caribbean, the Americas, Australia, New Zealand and South Africa are there to bare. For more information see www.barebeaches.com

French Atlantic coast

Formentera in Spain's Balearics

Golden sands in the Canaries

Timeless pleasures in Crete

One of hundreds in Croatia

Room for two in the Algarve

Bare chic in France

France, Britain's nearest neighbour, has bare bathing embedded in its culture. The country's tourist industry knows when it's on to a good thing and these days there are some fabulous resorts built around bare bathing. Yet more visitors simply turn up and get on with their skinny-dipping at any one of the dozens of nudist beaches around the coastline. Whether it's the sophistication of the Mediterranean or the solitude and sheer beauty of the never-ending beaches of the south-west that take your fancy, France offers a great choice of places to cast off your swimsuit.
More info at: www.naturisme.com.fr/pageplagesnaturistes.htm

Spain streaks ahead

Spain came to the bare beach party later than other holiday destinations but, oh boy, it's making up for lost time now. In just a single generation naked bathing has taken off. The Spanish, especially the younger generation, are now among the most enthusiastic and progressive advocates of the nude beach lifestyle. The mainland has a wealth of coves and secluded shores, plus some of the most popular nude beaches in the world. Offshore, each of the Balearic islands has something special to offer dedicated beachbums, particularly the small gem of an island Formentera, next to Ibiza, where going bare is second nature on most of its golden sandy beaches. For easy winter sun head for the Canaries where it's warm enough to strip off all year. As well as lovely beaches, there are more hotels (mostly 4- and 5-star) with dedicated nude sunbathing terraces than anywhere in the world.
More info at: www.naturismo.org

Greek classics

Greece feels as though time has stood still and is a clear favourite for lovers of pure relaxation. There are surprisingly few places where nude sunbathing is officially approved, but it's very popular, and the local tourist office is always happy to offer directions to the nearest clothes-optional beach. For the best skinny-dipping head out to the less crowded parts of the coast. Skiathos, Corfu, Kefalonia, Skopelos, Mykonos, Rhodes and Crete are just some of the islands of interest to travellers who enjoy bathing in their birthday suits.
More info at: www.geocities.com/HotSprings/1794

Croatia: beaches beyond count

Croatia is one of the hippest destinations around just now. Its lovely Adriatic coastline has more than 1,000 islands, where crystal

clear seas and bare beaches galore have drawn discerning holidaymakers for decades. There are literally hundreds of swimsuits-optional places dotted along the coast. Many hotels have their own nudist beach, or a public one nearby. The Brits have been more hesitant than other nationalities to take the plunge, but that is all set to change as more tour operators than ever are selling holidays to Croatia. Go before it loses that special charm.
More info at: www.cronatur.com

Portugal: space for every body

Portugal has some of Europe's finest coastline and the good news is it includes plenty of places to go bare. Many secluded beaches are empty, even on sunny days, so you can simply be yourself. The Algarve, on the southern coast, is the jewel in the crown for most holidaymakers. It's full of beautiful beaches, rocky inlets, hills, clifftops, cosmopolitan marinas with trendy cafes and designer shops, and plenty of hidden bays and fabulous coves where nude bathers gather. Portugal's capital, Lisbon, on the west coast, draws culture vultures rather than beach buffs. But even here there are now plenty of places nearby for back-to-nature bathing.
More info at: www.infolara.com/naturism/beaches.shtml

Pictured on the preceding pages, keen naturist couple Przemek and Joanna enjoy a holiday stroll by the sea. These two Polish naturists are keen to hear from others around the world; email: fansgolasy123@go2.pl

Club Holidays
at La Grande Cosse***
complete relaxation on the
Mediterranean Coast of France

Club Holidays

Luxurious mobile homes

Inclusive air and land packages or accommodation only

Regular excursions and activities

A warm welcome from Tim and Becky on site

La Grande Cosse***

3 star fully naturist site

3 swimming pools

3 kilometres of golden sandy beach

Camping and caravanning are also available.
Tel: 04 68 33 61 87 or contact@grandecosse.com

www.clubholidays.net   tel Ann on 01604 863300

If anywhere can, these 10 best nude beaches will put you off swimming costumes for life. All details are taken from Bare Beaches; see www.barebeaches.com

Handy sands in Miami

Popular sands at Vera Playa

Saharan sands at Maspalomas

1. Leucate Plage, France

Mediterranean coast, north of Perpignan
This superb bare beach has 1 km of fine golden sand, the classic Mediterranean beach. The water is normally calm and the shore shelves gently into the sea, making it popular with families. Three naturist resorts share the coastline but the beach is open to all and there's plenty of space for first-time skinny-dippers and lifelong nudists alike.

2. Plakias Beach, Crete, Greece

Plakias town, south-west Crete
A fabulous setting of cliffs, mountains and a huge sweep of golden sand make this beach a wonderful place for all-over tanning and fine snorkelling. The sea shelves gently, making it suitable for families, and there are showers available and umbrellas for hire. The nude area is the last section of the beach, to the left as you face the sea, often the busiest part of the bay.

3. Haulover Beach, USA

Sunny Isles, north of Miami's Bal Harbour
Situated in the south of the 'Sunshine State', this bare sandy beach has a huge following of visitors from across the globe. With glorious weather for most of the year and the vibrant city of Miami on the doorstep, it's not difficult to see why. The bare area is more than 800 yards long and has its own lifeguards. Refreshments, sunbeds and umbrellas are available.

4. Vera Playa, Spain

Costa Almeria, north of Garrucha
This is Spain's capital of bare bathing. The long wide sandy beach is popular in summer and has a wide choice of naturist accommodation. Beach bars, sunbeds, pedalos and yes, if you really want to try the naturist cliché, beach volleyball are all available. Almeria has the hottest and driest climate in the country, so the beach season is almost year-round.

5. Playa de Maspalomas, Canary Islands

Near Playa del Ingles, southern Gran Canaria
Hundreds of acres of sand dunes, looking just like the Sahara, frame the beautiful beach between Maspalomas and the popular resort of Playa del Ingles. It's 3 kms from one end to the other and over 1 km deep. The bare areas, like the swimsuited ones, have sunbeds and umbrellas for hire. For a quieter spot, walk into the vast expanse of dunes, but be careful not to get lost!

Vritomartis Hotel & Bungalows

on the coast of the South Cretan sea

Visit our web site
www.naturism-crete.com

Vritomartis Hotel
Hora Sfakion 73011
Crete, Greece

Phone: 00 30 2825091112
Fax: 00 30 2825091222
Email: vritnat@otenet.gr

The final five of our top 10 nude beaches around the world

Added attractions on Skiathos

Valalta, best in all Croatia

Happy days at Euronat; morning sun at Orient (pic by Rod Burkey)

6. Playa Es Pregons Gran, Balearic islands

Majorca south coast, north of Colonia Sant Jordi

This wonderful little bare bay has a perfect crescent of fine yellow sand, washed by a sea so transparent it looks like the Caribbean. There are no beach bars so bring your picnic and drinks. It's the jewel in the crown of the popular Es Trenc beach area, with many other places suitable for baring all nearby.

7. Banana Beach, Greece

Skiathos, near Koukounaries, on the south-west coast

Banana Beach is the collective name for three lovely sandy bays well loved by nude bathers. Before you ask, the name refers to the fact that the beaches are yellow and curved. During peak season bare bathers mainly use Little Banana, one of the smaller coves, as clothed holidaymakers descend on the main beach. Little Banana is often called the best bare beach in Greece, although there is plenty of competition for the accolade.

8. Valalta, Croatia

Istria, 5 miles from Rovinj

If you feel the need for a truly naked de-stress, Valalta is everything you could wish for. It's so good the nudist campsite here was voted the best in Croatia in 2004 – among all sites, not just bare ones. With 2 miles of sand and rock beaches, including secluded coves, lined by olive trees and vineyards, this nude beach and village are well loved by bare beach connoisseurs. Day visits cost 2 euro; info at: www.valalta.hr

9. Euronat, France

Atlantic coast, north-west of Bordeaux near Montalivet

The south-west coast of France is almost one vast nude beach, stretching over 100 miles from Biarritz to the Gironde. Among stiff competition, the nude resort beach of Euronat stands out for its clean golden sand, supervised swimming and friendly atmosphere. Thousands of happy families gather here, and the beach is open to both nudist campers and day visitors alike.

10. Orient Bay, St Martin

North-east coast of the Caribbean island

This mile-long sweep of white sand lapped by an aquamarine and turquoise sea is legendary among naked sun seekers as the ideal tropical treat. Club Orient naturist resort is at the southern end of the bay, which is the most popular section of beach for bare bathing. See www.cluborient.com for details on the many facilities.

Unwrap the world

Bare Beaches is the book that has got first-time skinny-dippers and lifelong naturists alike enthusing about the joys of bathing in the altogether. With hundreds of holiday ideas and pictures packed into its colourful pages. From glamourous beaches in the south of France to remote sands in the Caribbean, Bare Beaches makes nude beaches look as good as they feel

"This is the book your pale bits have been **waiting for**"
The Sunday Telegraph

"This is a great book... **a must read** for all avid naturists"
'Spanish' magazine

"The **world's best spots** for getting a brown bottom"
The Times

"Copiously illustrated with photographs, well designed with bright easy to read pages... **highly recommended**"
H&E Naturist

"Bare facts are supported with some **beautiful photography**"
Living Spain

"A lively, **modern** and professional guide" Naturist Life

Please use the order form below or copy the same information into a letter and send with your cheque to: Lifestyle Press, PO Box 1087, Bristol, BS48 3YD

UK orders only. For international prices and sales visit our website www.barebeaches.com

We're offering all Bare Britain readers the chance to buy our beautiful first book for **£12.95 post-free in the UK** direct from publisher Lifestyle Press. Simply choose one of the following to see what the world has to offer:

• Use or copy the coupon on the right
• Buy online at www.barebeaches.com
• Visit your local bookshop (available off the shelf or to order from Waterstone's, Borders and Books etc)

Or to order by phone simply call our orderline on **01733 385171**; the UK postal fee of **£2.00** applies to telesales.

Name...

Address..

....

....

Postcode..

Email (optional)..

Please send me........ copies of Bare Beaches
Price per copy is £12.95 with free UK postage

I enclose a cheque to Lifestyle Press Ltd for £............

If you want to try living naked for a week, nothing's better than the fully fledged naturist resorts listed here. Europe was the birthplace of naturism and has an astonishing array of naturist choices, including these dedicated facilities. See the websites for more details or see pages 194-195 for bare-friendly UK travel agents

France
- Club Oasis, Port Leucate
www.oasis-village.com
- Aphrodite Village, Port Leucate
www.leucatenature.com
- Cap d'Agde, Agde
www.capdagde.co.uk
- Arnaoutchot, Vielle-St-Girons
www.arna.com
- La Jenny, Le Porge
www.lajenny.fr
- Montalivet, Montalivet-les-Bains
www.chm-montalivet.com
- Euronat, Montalivet-les-Bains
www.euronat.fr
- Cap Natur, St Hilaire de Riez
www.cap-natur.com
- Belezy, Bedoin
www.belezy.com
- Sabliere, Barjac
www.campingsabliere.com
- Club Origan, near Nice
www.club-origan.com
- Riva Bella, Corsica
www.rivabella-corsica.com
- Piana Verde, Corsica
www.pianaverde.com
- La Chiappa, Corsica
www.chiappa.com

Spain
- Costa Natura, Estepona
www.costanatura.com
- Hotel Vera Playa, Vera Playa
www.hotelesplaya.com
- Vera Natura, Vera Playa
www.veranatura.com
- Bahia de Vera, Vera Playa
www.verabahia.com
- Torremar Natura, Vera Playa
www.naturistspain.com
- Natsun, Vera Playa
www.veraplaya.es
- Parque Vera, Vera Playa
www.veraplaya.info
- El Portus, Cartagena
www.elportus.com
- El Templo del Sol, L'Hospitalet
www.eltemplodelsol.com
- Relax-Nat, Palamos
www.campingrelaxnat.com
- Magnolias Natura, Gran Canaria
www.canariasnatura.com
- Charco del Palo, Lanzarote
www.charco-del-palo.com

Portugal
- Quinta da Horta, Ferragudo
www.naturist-holidays-portugal.com

Croatia
- Valalta, Rovinj
www.valalta.hr
- Koversada, Porec/Rovinj
www.istra.com/vrsar/eng/fkk.html
- Solaris, Porec
www.istra.com/porec/eng/fkk.html

Greece
- Vritomartis, Crete
www.naturism-crete.com

Holland
- Flevo-Natuur, Flevoland
www.flevonatuur.nl

Chalfont Holidays

specialising in quality naturist holidays

We offer holidays tailor made to your requirements to these naturist destinations, and will organise the most convenient flights for you (acting as retail agents for various ATOL operators), car hire, accommodation and travel insurance. We are members of the Travel Trust Association (R6530) which will safeguard the finances for your holiday, and we have an ATOL licence (T7062).

Lanzarote Castillo de Papagayo is the only naturist village in the Canary Islands enjoying a remote position on the north east coast of the island. We can arrange holidays in the full range of apartments and houses on this naturist estate. There are also a number of excellent textile hotels with nudist zones.

Gran Canaria Magnolias Natura is a new naturist centre that opened in 2004 well situated for the famous Maspalomas naturist beach. This is a small estate of self-catering bungalows set in a tropical garden around a beautiful pool with an excellent bar restaurant.

Fuerteventura This island has the most extensive and widely used sand beaches for naturism. We can offer self-catering accommodation and some beautiful textile hotels well situated for naturist beaches, including the new Occidental Grand which has a nudist area and pool and offers all inclusive holidays.

Tenerife In Tenerife there are a number of textile hotels with nudist zones, two with roof top swimming pools. We can also offer a self-catering apartment right next to the La Tejita naturist beach.

Crete The Hotel Vritomartis is the most idyllic naturist hotel we have yet discovered. Everything about the hotel and grounds is immaculate, and it has its own private naturist beach.

Spain Near J vea on the Costa Blanca there are two welcoming naturist guest houses offering bed and breakfast and a wonderful fully naturist experience. Both have nice gardens and pools, and one is available for rent in the summer months.

Austria At Ramsau in the Dachstein mountains this excellent naturist hotel provides a wonderful centre for winter snow sports and summer mountain walking.

Corsica This French island, 150 miles south-east of Nice, has the longest naturist beach in Europe, and Corsica has six naturist resorts to choose from. They offer different facilities and standards of accommodation but all enjoy beautiful sandy beaches and warm crystal clear sea water.

Turkey The Yacht Suzi Anna Naturist sailing holiday on an elegant yacht around the beautiful remote and mountainous southern coast of Turkey, flying to Dalaman, and based in the Gulf of Hisaronu, 25 miles from Marmaris.

Chalfont Holidays, c/o 196 High Road, Wood Green, London N22 8HH
Telephone: 01494 580 728 Email: info@chalfontholidays.co.uk
Website: www.chalfontholidays.co.uk

The Americas are taking to naturist holidays in a big way, with an emphasis on quality destinations for the discerning holidaymaker. The growing trend has prompted investment in some of the world's most modern and luxurious naturist accommodation.

The sun and sands of the Caribbean are a natural place to dispense with the swimming costume, and a popular winter sun destination. You can holiday naked at the resorts listed here, while many more resorts now have their own nude beaches on offer

USA
- Cypress Cove, Kissimmee, Fl
www.suncove.com
- Caliente Resort, Land O'Lakes, Fl
www.calienteresort.com
- Paradise Lakes, Land O'Lakes, Fl
www.paradiselakes.com
- Paradise Valley, Nr Atlanta, Ga
www.paradisevalleyresorts.com
- Desert Shadows, Palm Springs, Ca
www.desertshadows.com
- Terra Cotta, Palm Springs, Ca
www.sunnyfun.com

Caribbean
- Club Orient, St Martin
www.cluborient.com
- Sorobon Beach, Bonaire
www.sorobonbeachresort.com
(see advertisement on page 111)
- Firefly Beach Cottages, Jamaica
www.jamaicalink.com
- Eden Bay, Dominican Republic
www.edenbay.com
See Bare Beaches for full listings of Caribbean resorts which offer bare bathing facilities

Awaiting your email now
firefly@jamaicalink.com
Visit our website **jamaicalink.com** for full info
It's what you always promised yourself – and more

Firefly Beach Cottages
Negril Beach on the beautiful Caribbean
The ONLY clothes-optional hotel on famous
Negril Beach for naturists **&** their children
Established 25 years British/Jamaican family business
where guests return again and again
18 en-suite penthouse suites, apartments and studios
Phone: 00 1 876 957 4358   Fax: 00 1 876 957 3447
Mail: Firefly, P.O. Box 54, Negril, Jamaica
Beachfront — Beach Bar — Jacuzzi — Mini-gym
Tropical Garden and Birds
Book direct and fly direct from London or Manchester

DESERT SHADOWS INN
RESORT & VILLAS
Enjoy Palm Springs...au naturel!

where Sun & Fun
never ends!

Discover the difference of a world class nudist resort with the combined charm of a secluded inn and the luxury of a full service resort located in the heart of Palm Springs*, California. Desert Shadows Inn Resort & Villas offers **great rates** for daily, weekly & monthly holidays, whether you stay in our beautiful Hotel Rooms or in our sumptuous Villas.

*Palm Springs boasts an 87 degree yearly average temperature with 344 days of humidity-free sunshine per year.

go to www.desertshadows.com
or call 001 (760) 325-6410
& make your reservations today!

Visit our website for more information & to find out about upcoming events & celebrate with us...naturally!

Turkish Baths
www.harrogate.gov.uk/turkishbaths
Tel: 01423 556746

Center Parcs
www.centerparcs.co.uk
www.aquasana.co.uk
Tel: 01623 872921
Tel: 0870 6003008

Forestry Commission Wales
Tel: 01550 720394

Siva Relaxation Centre
www.sivarelaxation.com
(www.sivarelaxation.com/hours.htm
for costume-optional times)
RELAX@SivaRelaxation.com
Tel: 023 9286 2000

The Relaxation Centre
www.relaxationcentre.co.uk
enquiries@relaxationcentre.co.uk
Tel: 0117 970 6616

Strange as it seems to other Europeans, it is common for British spas and saunas to insist that you wear clothes, even for single-sex bathing. However, common sense prevails in a number of places, and although the places listed below aren't naturist as such, they do at least give you a chance to experience what a sauna, steam or spa experience is supposed to feel like. Some require clothes for mixed-sex sessions.

Turkish Baths, Harrogate

These newly refurbished baths, run by the local authority, are a fabulous spa facility which has recently been restored to full Victorian splendour. Built in a Moorish style, the baths require swimsuits to be worn for mixed-sex sessions. For times of single sex-sessions see the website or contact the baths.

Center Parcs, UK-wide

Center Parcs is a chain of holiday resorts with an adults-only 'Aqua Sana' spa facility. The rules allow for 'natural choice' at times, which means clothing optional. Reports on the NUFF website (www.nuff.org.uk) confirm that naturists often enjoy the spas, although many and sometimes all other users might prefer to stay dressed. Check with the centres for up to date information. There are four Aqua Sana centres: Oasis Whinfell Forest, Cumbria; Elveden Forest, Suffolk; Sherwood Forest, Nottinghamshire; and Longleat Forest, Wiltshire.

Forest sauna, Llandovery, Carmarthenshire

The Forestry Commission Wales has developed a sauna facility near Llandovery in Carmarthenshire. Set in secluded and attractive woodland, it can accomodate up to 10 bathers. The sauna is heated by a woodburning stove and there is a stream nearby but bathers are encouraged to use the purpose built plunge pool. It is available for group bookings and the cost is £60 for a three-hour morning or afternoon session. For further information or to book contact the Forestry Commission.

Siva Relaxation Centre, Southsea

This venue has clothing-optional times, listed on the website.

The Relaxation Centre, Bristol

Clothing is optional at this lovely spa centre in Bristol during women-only sessions and once a week for couples-only sessions. Regular mixed sessions require costumes; click on 'Opening hours' on the website for full information.

It's not just the French and Spanish who can enjoy overnight stays at naturist centres. The UK has a huge range of choices, helped by the fact that many of the country's clubs welcome genuine **naturist holidaymakers**. The list below includes some places for those who like to unwind away from home with nothing on.

The list is divided into sites that make a particular feature of their holiday facilities, and those where facilities are often available. Other clubs may also welcome holiday visitors; see the full **club listings** on pages 116-191 for site details.

You will need to contact any site first to enquire about availability and **check entry requirements**. Many sites restrict entry to members of British Naturism or other naturist organisations or clubs. All of them take care to ensure all visitors and members respect the friendly and genuine **naturist ethos**.

Main naturist holiday centres

- Carbeil Holiday Park, Cornwall page 119
- Little Crugwallins, Cornwall page 120
- Roselan, Cornwall page 123
- St Annes, Dorset page 123
- Southleigh Manor, Cornwall page 125
- South Hants Country Club, Hampshire page 138
- Broadlands, Norfolk page 147
- Croft Country Club, Norfolk page 149
- Merryhill Leisure, Norfolk page 151
- Pevors Farm Cottages, Essex/Suffolk page 153
- Spielplatz, Hertfordshire page 156
- Tything Barn, Pembrokeshire page 181

Naturist clubs with holiday facilities

- Tara, Gloucs page 125
- Wyvern, Gloucs page 127
- Aztec, West Sussex page 129
- BDOC, Hants page 130
- Diogenes, Buckinghamshire page 131
- Heritage Club, Berkshire page 133
- Invicta, Kent page 134
- The Naturist Foundation, Kent page 134
- Shabden Leisure Circle, Kent/East Sussex page 137
- Valerian Sun Club, Isle of Wight page 141
- Blackthorns, Bedfordshire page 147
- Cambridge Outdoor Club, Cambs page 148
- Springwood, Essex page 158
- Charnwood Acres, Leicestershire page 161

Naturist clubs with holiday facilities (cont.)

- East Midland Sunfolk, Lincolnshire page 162
- Nottingham Sun Club, Nottinghamshire page 163
- Sungrove, Lincolnshire page 164
- Telford Naturist Club, Shropshire page 165
- Ashdene, West Yorkshire page 167
- Valley Club, North Yorkshire page 168
- White Rose Club, North Yorkshire page 169
- Yorkshire Sun Society, East Yorkshire page 169

- Lakeland Outdoor Club, Cumbria page 171
- Liverpool Sun and Air, Merseyside page 172
- Manchester Sun and Air, Cheshire page 173
- Ribble Valley Club, Lancashire page 175
- Solway Sun Club, Cumbria page 176
- Western Sunfolk, Monmouthshire page 182
- Scottish Outdoor Club, Loch Lomond page 185
- Sunnybroom, near Aberdeen page 186

SOROBON BEACH RESORT
Bonaire, Dutch Antilles

Naturism on a Caribbean island

Sorobon is a small family oriented naturist resort with a magnificent private beach by the Caribbean Sea. Ideal for swimming, snorkelling, diving and windsurfing. Gentle trade winds ensure there is always a cool spot in the heat of the day. You will have splendid views across the bay and sea, a constant changing of colors: green, deep-blue, turquoise. Chalets with all conveniences: sittingroom and bedroom, airconditioning, kitchen, spacious terrace. Including maid service, linens and towels. Snorkel equipment, kayaks, petanque field, table tennis, yoga and massage. Enjoy the parakeets, flamingoes, birds, iguanas, all pure nature..!

Tel: 00-599 717 8080
Fax: 00-599 717 6080
Please visit our extended website at
www.sorobon.co.uk

Picture previous page taken at **Rivendell** naturist club (see page 122) by Charlie Simonds of Parafotos films (www.parafotos.co.uk)

Do not expect

Luxury facilities and on-site staff (only a few commercial sites have them)

An immediate answer to enquiries, especially if the club is run by members on a volunteer basis

To be confronted by any sexual activity

To turn up and gain entry on the day

To see cameras, or hear music players without personal headphones

What is a naturist club?

There is nothing quite like a good old-fashioned British naturist club anywhere in the world. These islands of unclothed freedom have been lovingly built and maintained by their members since the first pioneers of the 1930s. Tucked away in some of the most beautiful and peaceful corners of the countryside, they continue to offer a unique haven for back-to-nature relaxation.

They are not places where members go simply in order to be naked. Rather, they are designed around activities best done without clothes: swimming in the club pool, taking a sauna or simply sunbathing. The facilities often rival the best a local sports centre could offer but at a fraction of the cost and within a more natural environment.

Protecting their privacy

Many members are attracted by the privacy of a naturist club. They know that they and their families are safe in the company of like-minded people: the club knows everyone inside its gates. Some guard their sanctuary with unwavering dedication, scrutinising newcomers closely and fighting shy of any publicity.

Traditionalists say such discretion is essential to preserving the naturist ethos from intrusion from the outside world. Others say the clubs are simply being too coy. Some beach naturists shun the tight-knit communities in favour of freedom and solitude by the sea. Even the names tell of an age that is perhaps passing, when naturists hid behind the euphemisms of 'outdoor club', 'sun association', 'members' club' and, most common of all, 'sun club'.

Certainly outside the club gates the world has grown accustomed to the fact that naturism has existed throughout living memory. Public tolerance of genuine naturism has grown to such a point that even the government amends laws to make allowance for it. And 98% of Britons are happy for naturism to be allowed in some form (an NOP poll in 2001 found that just 2% of adults said naturism should be illegal).

Many clubs have modernised and take pride in promoting their new pools and spa complexes, tennis courts and holiday pitches. The average club lies somewhere in the middle, working hard to make their clubs attractive to new and existing members, while taking great care to preserve a genuine naturist atmosphere.

Who goes bare?

It's hard to generalise about who goes to naturist clubs. The most common age group at most clubs is middle-aged but you can easily meet a student or a great-grandmother. The most common professions among UK naturists are teaching, nursing and healthcare, but you could meet a vicar, a plumber or a high court judge.

It doesn't matter when the clothes are off and the sun's shining. But one common feature does unite naturist clubs: they tend to stress the family atmosphere. Many club naturists say they prefer to keep their naturist activities to their private grounds rather than a public beach. Naturists work hard to make sure their clubs are a safe, secluded and convenient place to bring families. It's common to find members who have been going to a club all their lives, and who bring their own children and grandchildren along.

It is important to remember that most naturist clubs are owned and run by their members rather than an individual owner. This usually means they have no resident staff so you need to arrange visits in advance to make sure there's someone there. The rules and practices of member-owned clubs are more like the sort of customs people have in their own private homes, handed down from generation to generation.

Swimming clubs

There are around 100 swimming pools across the country that go naturist for special evenings. Ranging from small local pools to vast leisure centres, these events attract a strong following of regular visitors and are an easy way to try skinny-dipping without the hassle of finding a beach or the commitment and cost of joining a full naturist club. Swimming club organisers ask for some form of ID at the door as reassurance that they know who everyone is. British Naturism membership is an acceptable form of ID in many places (see page 6).

Giving something back

All clubs encourage their members to help look after the place, but the days of earnest men wearing nothing but wellingtons as they dig out drainage ditches are several generations ago. Apart from the fact that people don't volunteer their spare time like they used to, naturist clubs have been established for a long time in Britain. The groundwork has long since finished, the grounds and plants are mature and simply need ongoing love and care.

In our fast-moving world, naturist clubs continue to offer an escape that is almost too simple to explain. The timeless pleasure of immersing yourself in nature just as you were born can only really be understood through experience alone.

Do expect

Remote rural locations with simple facilities and a genuine back-to-nature feel

People sitting on towels when they use a chair or bench

A very strong community spirit

Traditions and rules that have developed over many decades

People staying dressed when it's cold

To become a member for life once you find a club you like!

Bare places

South West   118-127
Bath/Bristol, Cornwall, Devon, Dorset, Gloucestershire, Somerset, Wiltshire

South East   128-143
Berkshire, Buckinghamshire, East Sussex, Hampshire, Isle of Wight, Kent,
Oxfordshire, Surrey, West Sussex

Eastern   144-159
Bedfordshire, Cambridgeshire, Essex, Hertfordshire, Norfolk, Suffolk

East and West Midlands   160-165
Birmingham, Leicestershire, Lincolnshire, Northamptonshire, Nottinghamshire,
Shropshire, Staffordshire, Warwickshire

Yorkshire   166-169
East Yorkshire, North Yorkshire, South Yorkshire, West Yorkshire

North West   170-177
Cheshire, Cumbria, Greater Manchester, Lancashire, Merseyside

North East   178-179
Newcastle upon Tyne

Wales   180-183
Gwynedd, Monmouthshire, Pembrokeshire, West Glamorgan

Scotland, Ireland   184-187
Edinburgh, Loch Lomond, Glasgow, Aberdeen, Tayside, Dumfries and
Galloway, Belfast

National clubs   188-191

The suitably French sport of boules is
frequently played in Britain's naturist
clubs, such as the **White House** in
Surrey, pictured right on a spring day

South West

Aquasol Swimming Club

Knowle, Bristol
This naturist group meets weekly for a one-hour swim on Wednesdays from 7.30pm to 8.30pm. The club uses the Jubilee pool in Knowle.

Carbeil Holiday Park

Downderry, near Torpoint, Cornwall
Tucked into a beautiful Cornish valley, Carbeil is one of the UK's select naturist holiday parks, welcoming visitors to enjoy its pool and accommodation au naturel. It's registered with the English Tourist Board and has three AA penants.

A family-run site, the park is just 10 minutes' walk from a naturist beach and has plenty of information about other naturist beaches and regular holiday attractions nearby.

Among the facilities are an outdoor swimming pool, table tennis, children's play area and barbeque areas. There is a bar and servery where breakfast, snacks and main meals are served and picnic benches dotted around the site. Tents, campervans and caravans are accommodated and there are full washing, cleaning, laundry and disposal facilities on site, as well as hook-up points.

Far West

St Austell and Redruth, Cornwall
Given the wonderful naturist beaches in the area, it's hardly surprising locals have a swimming club to continue their naturist leisure throughout the year. Members meet twice a month, using two different centres for swimming and socialising. The club takes a break during the holiday months of July, August and December.

At Polkyth Leisure Centre in St Austell, where members meet on the second Saturday of the month, there is a full-size pool, squash and badminton courts, a spa pool, sauna and hydrotherapy pool. Members gather in the bar afterwards to catch up.

The Penventon Hotel in Redruth, where the club gathers on the fourth Saturday of the month, has a beautiful pool suite in classical Greek style. Visitors and potential members are invited to get in touch to find out more.

Larches

Exeter, Devon and Street, Somerset
This naturist swimming club meets in two locations for regular swimming and sauna sessions. In Exeter the club uses the

Aquasol
Tel: 0117 909 6058 (call before 8.30pm)

Carbeil Holiday Park
Treliddon Lane, Downderry, Torpoint, Cornwall PL11 3LS
Tel: 01503 250 636

Far West
Tel: 07891 256130
www.farwestnaturist.org.uk
farwestinfo@hotmail.com

Larches
Tel: 01392 215585
Tel: 01823 270252
larches64@ukonline.co.uk

Carbeil Holiday Park, picture supplied by the centre

Rivendell, opposite, is one of the South West's many well-equipped and popular naturist clubs. Picture opposite top by Charlie Simonds (www.parafotos.co.uk) and picture bottom supplied by the club

Little Crugwallins
Rosemary & Rupert Adkins, Little
Crugwallins, Burngullow, St Austell
PL26 7TH
Tel: 01726 63882
www.littlecrug-naturism.co.uk
rupertadkins@onetel.com

Marlborough and District NC
Tel: 07092 031130
www.madnat.org
info@madnat.org

The Pickwick Club
Tel: 01225 811690
roy.roach@zoom.co.uk

The Pines Outdoor Club
Tel: 07753 117669
www.pines1972.co.uk
the.pinesoc@virgin.net

Ridgewood Sun Club
Tel: 07977 518930
www.gordons.demon.co.uk/ridgewood
bob@ridgewoodbob1.fsbusiness.co.uk
gray-ridgewood@tiscali.co.uk

The Pines Outdoor Club, below, is
the place for back-to-nature naturism

Pyramids Swimming and Leisure Centre, and in Street members gather at the Strode Pool. Visitors are welcome; contact the club for more information.

Little Crugwallins

Near St Austell, Cornwall
This much-praised naturist retreat is set in a 5-acre smallholding. Situated in central Cornwall, it's handy for attractions such as the Eden Project and Lost Gardens of Heligan, as well as Cornwall's many fine naturist beaches. The unofficially naturist Vault beach is 10 miles away.

The site itself has a spa pool and three lawns for sunbathing. It's surrounded by trees and fields and you can go naked throughout the gardens and grounds apart from on the access drive.

There are three accommodation units to rent, two with two bedrooms and one with a single bedroom. Units are well equipped and although converted from industrial use are comfortable and have views over the gardens and fields.

Marlborough and District Naturist Club

Marlborough, Wiltshire
Using the cheerful nickname 'Madnat', this group of naturists enjoys clothes-free recreation at the Marlborough Leisure Centre.

Meeting every two weeks or so, visitors and members can use the swimming pool, sauna, steam room, badminton courts and other facilities. Professional yoga classes are also available.

The club has held innovative women-only introductory sessions in the past to reassure female newcomers of what naturism is about. The club welcomes visiting families and British Naturism members – contact them for details, or if you're interested in membership.

The Pickwick Club

Corsham, Wiltshire
The Pickwick Club is a swimming group which hires out a local pool, sauna, spa pool and steam room for naturist events.

Visitors are welcome with prior notice.

The Pines Outdoor Club

Forest of Dean, Gloucestershire
The beauty and tranquillity of this club at the heart of the Forest of Dean have much to

offer naturists in seach of some back-to-nature relaxation. Its secluded location means there is no pool or electricity but the natural attractions more than compensate.

Members enjoy regular social gatherings including barbeques on the sunbathing lawn.

Activities include beautiful woodland walks and a boules court. The site accommodates tents but access is unsuitable for caravans or large campers.

The club welcomes visitors for a day or a weekend trip to share the peace and tranquillity or take part in a barbeque.

Little Crugwallins has holiday accommodation overlooking the beautiful farm and woodland setting. Picture below supplied by the club

Ridgewood Sun Club

Clevedon, Somerset

This is a small club run by its members in the Somerset countryside. There is a club house, miniten and boules, and a splash pool for cooling off on summer days.

The club holds regular social events and trips to other naturist sites.

Little Crugwallins

Mid Cornwall, near Eden Project

Naturist self-catering accommodation in our tastefully furnished cottages sleeping 2 or 5
- Extensive secluded gardens
- Luxurious indoor Jacuzzi
- Full central heating
- Easy access to north and south coasts
- Low season short breaks

Rosemary & Rupert Adkins
Little Crugwallins Farm,
Burngullow, St Austell PL26 7TH
Tel or fax 01726 63882

email rupertadkins@onetel.com
www.littlecrug-naturism.co.uk

Rivendell
Tel: 01202 824013
www.rivendell-naturism.co.uk

Rivendell

Wimborne, Dorset

It's not just the name that bears a close resemblance to the elves' retreat in the Lord of the Rings. Like Tolkien's fantasy hideaway, Rivendell is also a place of relaxation and natural beauty. The name actually refers to a piece of land split in two by a stream, which also rings true of Rivendell's 5-acre site.

The club is a conservation area, with many rare flowers including orchids growing around the natural grounds. Wild deer wander through the woodland and grassy glades, where naturists sunbathe in the summer. There's a lake where you can sit and look at the kingfishers tracking their prey.

Aside from the natural attractions, there is a grass miniten court, boules and table tennis, while giant size Jenga or draughts keep visitors amused.

Further facilities include the club's heated swimming pool and 8-person spa pool, a sauna and a conservatory-style clubhouse and restaurant.

It's a charming place and naturist-minded visitors are assured of a warm welcome; bookings must be made by contacting the club in advance.

Rivendell, below and opposite top, has a lake where kingfishers play and naturists unwind. Pictures below left and opposite by Charlie Simonds of naturist film maker Parafotos (www.parafotos.co.uk), picture below right supplied by the club

Roselan

Newquay, Cornwall

Roselan is a private guest house set in two acres near the north coast of Cornwall, about 3 miles from the unofficial naturist beach by Perranporth. The house is a large country cottage with open beamed ceilings and log fires.

The house and south-facing gardens are secluded enough to enjoy a totally naturist stay. Members of the Far West naturist club visit the place regularly to enjoy the swimming pool and the wood-burning Finnish sauna and spa bath, available for a small charge. A wide range of complementary therapies are offered including massage, stress counselling, diet and nutrition advice, therapeutic hypnosis and psychotherapy. Costs are available on request.

There are camping facilities available or two fully equipped three berth caravans for hire. For a brochure and other information call the club and they will be happy to try to help.

St Annes

Near Wimborne, Dorset

This naturist camping and carvanning site is in the ideal location for a holiday on the south coast of England. Close to Bournemouth and the popular Studland Bay naturist beach, St Annes attracts naturist visitors looking for comfort and seclusion.

There are three camping fields set amid woodland, with full facilities including free showers. It even has a quiet corner where people who are new to naturism can discover the pleasures of going naked in their own space. Caravans, tents and campervans are all accommodated. Contact the site to make a reservation.

Roselan
Tel: 01872 572765

St Annes
Reg and Hazel Russell, St Annes Cottage, Horton Road, Three Legged Cross, Nr Wimborne, Dorset BH21 6SD
Tel: 01202 825529
stannescottage1@aol.com

RIVENDELL The place to be seen in

This very special club has so much to offer the true naturist, who likes friendliness and natural surroundings, with all the modern amenities of a modern leisure centre.

The **heated swimming pool**, 10-seater **hot tub**, **sauna**, **club house** and **restaurant** are all situated around a large south facing patio – just right for that **all-over tan**.

For more details please contact
'RIVENDELL', Wimborne, Dorset BH21 7JN
Tel: 01202 824013
info@rivendell-naturism.co.uk   www.rivendell-naturism.co.uk

With five acres of landscaped grounds, lake, boules courts, table tennis and volleyball... it makes sense to join Rivendell!

Severn Vale
Tel: 01452 522896
Tel: 01453 873689
www.svsc.fsworld.co.uk
secretary@svsc.fsworld.co.uk

South Western
Tel: 07884 330734
hilary-mbush@supanet.com

Southleigh Manor
Bob and Kathy Prescott, Southleigh
Manor holiday club, St Columb Major,
Cornwall TR9 6HY
Tel: 01637 880938
www.southleigh-manor.com
enquiries@southleigh-manor.com

Southleigh Manor, below, is a superb
base for a holiday in Cornwall. Picture
by Charlie Simonds of naturist film
maker Parafotos (www.parafotos.co.uk)

Severn Vale Swimming Club

Tewkesbury, Gloucestershire

This naturist group enjoys the run of a local leisure centre two or
three evenings a month. With two pools, a grotto, spa pool, steam
room, sauna and gym on offer, the swims are also a chance for
members and visitors to socialise throughout the year.

Visitors and potential members need to contact the club in
advance, although members of British Naturism and other INF
bodies can turn up if they have their cards.

South Western Outdoor Club

Evershot, Dorset

This members club has a 4-acre site surrounded by Dorset
woodland, developed over the past 40 years to include a club
house, sunbathing lawns and games courts plus a children's play
area. Visitors are welcome but must contact the club for details.

Southleigh Manor Holiday Club

St Columb, mid Cornwall

Southleigh Manor is a holiday and local naturist club situated in
4 acres of beautiful gardens. It describes itself as a place of peace
and tranquillity with a
welcoming family atmosphere
for members and guests alike.

Its location is ideal for
holidays, making it a popular
place with tourists. There is a
licensed bar with dining area
offering home-cooked food.
Bathing and sunbathing are
based around the extensive
lawns, outdoor heated pool
and paddling pool, large sun
room, sunbed, sauna and
Jacuzzi. Visitors can arrange a
de-stressing massage from
Kathy, a qualified masseuse.

Games include a pool table,
darts board, mini golf, table
tennis, children's play area and
a volleyball/badminton area.
Petanque games and barbeques
are held weekly in the summer,
plus quiz and curry nights, race
nights and themed discos.

Visitors looking for a naturist holiday or a day visit are welcome and should call first to arrange. Accommodation includes 50 pitches with electric hook-ups for caravans, motorhomes and tents. There are two luxury self-contained log cabins (for up to six people) for hire as well as some two- and four-berth touring caravans. Facilities include a toilet block with showers, sinks, shaver points and a hair dryer, plus a laundry room with all facilities and a covered washing up area.

Members of the club can use the facilities seven days a week during the summer season, which usually starts at Easter. Club night is on a Friday and runs throughout the year.

Tara

Chipping Sodbury, Cotswolds, Gloucestershire
A beautiful woodland is home to this 7-acre naturist haven, attracting local members and holidaymakers alike. Situated within easy reach of the M4 and M5, Tara promotes itself as a base for exploring the Cotswolds, Forest of Dean, Bath, Gloucester and Weston-super-Mare.

Tara
Send SAE for brochure, price list or membership details to: Tara, Mapleridge Lane, Chipping Sodbury, Gloucestershire BS37 6PB
Tel: 01454 294256

Tara, below, is an ideal holiday base

The premier naturist site central to the whole of Cornwall. We are less than 30 minutes from two well-used naturist beaches. The Eden Project and Camel Cycle Trail are within easy reach by car.

SOUTHLEIGH MANOR
NATURALLY

Affiliated to the CCBN

AA 3 Pennant Family Park

RECOMMENDED BY THE ALAN ROGERS GUIDE

Southleigh has been created especially for the naturist on holiday.
We are a family centre with fully equipped luxury log cabins and touring caravans for hire.
50 pitches with or without hook-up for caravans, tents and motorhomes.

• Victorian licensed bar and comfortable dining area
• Home cooked food
• Large conservatory
• Small shop (open in high season)

Contact: Bob and Kathy, Southleigh Manor Holiday Club, St. Columb Major, Cornwall TR9 6HY Tel: 01637 880938
Email: enquiries@southleigh-manor.com
Web: www.southleigh-manor.com

• Heated swimming and paddling pool
• Jacuzzi, sauna and sun bed
• Children's playground
• Mini golf, table tennis and volleyball net

If you live in Cornwall why not join Southleigh Manor Sun Club?

Torbay Sun Club
Tel: 07786 227242
www.torbaysunclub.co.uk
info@torbaysunclub.co.uk

"Our aim is to provide a naturist centre where all can unwind from the stress and strain of every-day life," as the club puts it. And the facilities have been developed to do just that. With an outdoor and an indoor pool, sauna and well-developed holiday pitches, Tara takes particular pride in the upkeep of its grounds.

While built for relaxation like all naturist clubs, Tara also has a range of sports facilities including miniten, volleyball, badminton, boules, croquet and even a nine-hole pitch and putt course. There are barbeque areas, lawns and patio for sitting and sunbathing and inside the pavilion a pool table, darts, table tennis, refreshments and a TV with video and DVD.

A new block with all amenties, including disabled access and laundry room, has just been added. Holidaymakers are well catered for with 14 hard-standing, hooked-up pitches for caravans and motorhomes, eight sites for tents, and one self-catering holiday bungalow available to visitors staying a week or more.

Holiday visitors staying a night or more are welcome from March to October, and should contact the club in advance, as should anyone wishing to join.

Torbay Sun Club

Totnes and Paignton, Devon
Torbay Sun Club lacks a permanent site but more than makes up for it with plenty of naturist swimming, social and other events in the area. With around 200 members ageing from 0 to well over 80, it prides itself on being friendly and inclusive. Activities are disabled- and family-friendly.

The club holds swimming and sauna events at Totnes, while the venue in Paignton has a sauna, steam room and Jacuzzi. In addition to anyone living locally, visitors on holiday in the area are also invited to get in touch.

TARA

Ideal touring base for: Bath, Bristol, Gloucs, Cotswolds, Wales, Forest of Dean, Cheddar, Weston-Super-Mare

Hilary and Allan welcome you to the tranquil and unique atmosphere of Tara. In a beautiful woodland setting with well-groomed lawns, the club has much to offer the holiday maker.

We are open from March to the end of October. Limited facilities at beginning and end of season. Please send SAE for brochure and membership info to:
**TARA, Mapleridge Lane, Chipping Sodbury, South Gloucs BS37 6PB
Tel: 01454 294256**

- Touring/camping sites
- Electric hook-ups
- Super pitches
- New shower/toilet block with facilities for the disabled
- Heated indoor swimming pool
- Outdoor pool
- Sunbathing lawns

- Recreational facilities
- 2 new miniten courts
- 9-hole pitch and putt course
- Seasonal pitches
- Annual membership
- Holiday bungalow sleeps 2
- Easy reach M5 and M4
- Note no pets allowed

Two Rivers

North Devon

This naturist swimming club meets in Torrington once a month for a swim and sauna. A small but friendly group, they require visitors to be a member of British Naturism (see page 6) or another naturist club before visiting.

Members also organise social events during the year.

Wimborne Sun Club

Wimborne, Dorset

"We are a friendly group of people who meet for swimming and chatting," say the organisers of this regular naturist swimming session in the Dorset town.

With both a weekly swim at the Queen Elizabeth Leisure Centre and monthly visits to Rivendell, the nearby naturist club, members have plenty of opportunity for naturist activity.

Visitors are very welcome with ID or British Naturism cards.

Wyvern Swim and Sun Club

Near Ledbury, Gloucs/Herefordshire border

"Cast away your clothes and your cares and enjoy our beautiful rural setting," is Wyvern's welcoming cry. The club has 4 acres of peaceful grounds to do just that, and also organises monthly swimming at a local pool. It's one of the few naturist clubs in the UK with a superb view, and has been attracting naturists since 1983. It takes pride in its friendly, family atmosphere, with a wide range of facilities to keep members happily occupied.

Several lawns for sunbathing, a children's play area, a well-equipped clubhouse, woodland walks, boules and badminton courts and a barbecue area have been added over the years. More importantly for those wishing to stay are the camping and motorhome pitches, available to members and visiting holidaymakers from May to September. Caravans can not be accommodated.

Once a month Wyvern hosts a naturist swim at the Cascades swimming pool in Tewkesbury.

Prospective members and other visitors to the club or swim are very welcome and should call in advance.

Two Rivers
Tel: 07792 259878
http://beehive.thisisnorthdevon.co.uk
(a search for 'naturist' will find the club)
tobysgarden@aol.com

Wimborne Sun Club
Tel: 01258 857143
www.wimbornesunclub.org
secretary@wimbornesunclub.org

Wyvern Swim and Sun Club
Tel: 07754 417810
www.wyvernsun.com
wyvernssc@fsmail.net
wyvern.sun@wyvernsun.com

Wyvern's superb open views are a rare treat in UK naturist clubs, making the most of the beautiful rural setting for outdoor leisure

South East

Adventurers

Hucking, near Sittingbourne, Kent

Adventurers prides itself on being a friendly, family club. The main facilities lie in a clearing at the heart of eight acres of woodland.

An outdoor swimming pool and pine-clad sauna provide plenty of naturist relaxation, while a volleyball court and petanque area provide the games. There is also has club house and children's play area, with woodland walks winding through the trees.

Visitors are welcome to camp on the club's five free pitches; contact the club to arrange a visit.

Avonvale

Ringwood, Hampshire

Avonvale lies amid ancient woodland in the New Forest, close to Ringwood and handy for Studland naturist beach. The 5-acre club, which is owned by the members, prides itself on a beautiful forest setting and friendly atmosphere.

It includes a large pavilion with kitchen, sauna and outdoor swimming pool, two miniten and two petanque courts, a barbeque area and children's play area, enclosed for safety. There are many lawns for sunbathing, including areas set aside for members to camp. The club enjoys an active social life. During the course of the year members can take part in a skittles evening with pub dinner, a fun sports weekend, themed food evenings, a cabaret night and sauna evenings on Fridays in the winter.

The club has been going for 45 years and takes great care in protecting its unique plants and wildlife; it has links to the local badger and bat groups. The grounds also have paths suitable for mountain biking and nature trails.

The club is open all year and cherishes a reputation for making new members feel a welcome part of its naturist community.

Aztec Sun Club

Crawley, West Sussex

A place to get away from it all, and yet handy for Crawley and the Gatwick area, Aztec is a naturist haven for more than 200 members. With 5 acres of grounds and good facilities, the members enjoy a busy social life.

The heated indoor pool is open from April to October, and is complemented by a sauna and spa pool. Back on dry land, sports facilities include two miniten courts, volleyball and badminton courts and four boules courts. There are lawns for

---

Adventurers
50 The Ferns, Larkfield, Aylesford, Kent ME20 6NF
Tel: 01732 840909
www.adventurers.btinternet.co.uk
adventurers@btinternet.com

Avonvale
Tel: 01202 821362
Tel: 07904 267705
www.avonvalesunclub.co.uk
ray.bryant99@btinternet.com

Aztec
The secretary, Hollywood, Copthorne Way, Copthorne, West Sussex RH10 3RX
Tel: 01293 882171
www.aztecsunclub.co.uk
secretary@aztecsunclub.co.uk

Aztec Sun Club has 5 acres for both relaxation and naturist leisure, with facilities pictured opposite top and below by Charlie Simonds, of Parafotos (www.parafotos.co.uk). Pictured opposite bottom, **Avonvale** lies amid ancient woodland; picture supplied by the club

Barton Swim Club
Tel: 023 8090 5935
jjohnver@aol.com

BDOC
Matchams Drive, Matchams Lane,
Matchams, Ringwood, Hants BH24 2BU
Tel: 01425 472121
Tel: 02380 738034
www.bdoc.co.uk

Bracknell Sauna-Swim Club
Tel: 0118 966 3432
www.bracknell.freeuk.com
spat1@compuserve.com

Aztec, below, has plenty to keep you entertained. Picture by Charlie Simonds

sunbathing and playing other games, and a barbeque area. Midday meals are normally available on summer weekends.

For those wishing to have a holiday, the site has room for 25 caravans or motorhomes and 20 tents. Although there are no water or electrical hook-ups, holidaymakers can use the club's shower and laundry facilities, and a disposal point is available. Visitors are very welcome and should make arrangements in advance.

Barton Swim Club
Barton on Sea, Hampshire
This friendly naturist club meets on the last Saturday of the month for an evening of swimming and relaxing. Its members also hold regular social events throughout the year. With a pool, sauna, steam room and spa pool to enjoy from 5.45pm to 7.45pm, the club invites visitors and potential members to get in touch.

Bournemouth and District Outdoor Club
Ringwood, Hampshire
With 5 acres of grounds set in woodland clearings, BDOC says it is a delight for any nature lover, especially naturist ones. It's close to the Avon Heath Country Park and handy as a holiday base for surrounding attractions such as Studland naturist beach and the New Forest.

There are long-term plans to develop the site, which already has a 25-foot free-standing swimming pool and a marquee clubhouse, plus a boules area, a children's play area and a patio.

The club is geared to members, with regular social events, but has some tent and caravan sites, with hook-ups, for holiday visitors during the summer. Advance bookings must be made. Visitors have a huge choice of nearby restaurants, inns and tearooms and holiday choices include the family fun centre at Moors Valley Country Park and a dry-run ski slope.

Bracknell Sauna-Swim Club
Bracknell, Berkshire
This group meets on Sundays to enjoy all the spa and sauna facilities of a local sports centre "with no soggy cossies clinging to your body". Among the attractions are the sauna, hot tub, whirl pool, steam room and lounge area. Visitors who are members of British Naturism (see page 6) are welcome to get in touch.

Diogenes

Rickmansworth/Chalfont St Peter, Bucks

Diogenes, a club owned by its members, has six acres of landscaped grounds packed with all the facilities a naturist could hope for. It describes itself as a "little piece of heaven in the countryside", providing a retreat from the rigours of daily life.

It's accessible enough to attract many of its 300 members from London and around. There's an active social life around the club, with a social or sports event held every couple of weeks.

It has used its present site for more than 40 years and has a wide range of activities. These include an outdoor and indoor pool, a sauna suite, a children's play area, boules courts, miniten courts, a large lawn for sunbathers, a woodland walk and a green pond, all based around a large country house. Holiday visitors are welcome but must make arrangements first. There is plenty of space for tents and motor homes, and many pitches have electric hook ups.

Four Seasons

Henfield, West Sussex

Describing itself as a "lovely sun club set in 5 acres of very sheltered grounds," Four Seasons has both the facilities and social

Diogenes
Freepost SL827, Gerrards Cross,
Buckinghamshire SL9 0BR
www.diogenessunclub.co.uk
contact_diogenes@hotmail.com

Four Seasons
Tel: 01903 245537
www.rholmwood.freeserve.co.uk
bigjohnfs@amserve.com

The house and pool lie at the heart of **Diogenes**. Picture by the club

Looking for an escape from the rigours of daily life?

DIOGENES SUN CLUB is a little piece of heaven in the Buckinghamshire countryside, around an hour from Central London.

Relax or be active, as you choose. Our six acres of landscaped grounds around our large country house features outdoor pool, indoor pool, sauna suite, children's play area, boules courts, miniten courts, large sunbathing lawn and woodland walks. There are sports and social events throughout the year and plenty of space for tents and motor homes for those who can't tear themselves away or want a base to explore the Chiltern Hills, Windsor, Oxford and London.

Come and see why the naturists at Diogenes are among the happiest in the land.

Visit www.diogenessunclub.co.uk or write to
Freepost SL 827, Gerrards Cross, SL9 0BR
for more information

Halcyon
Tel: 023 92 388482

Haslemere Sun Club
Tel: 01730 893223
www.sunnyacres.co.uk
memsec@hsclub.idps.co.uk

Bare bathers making the most of a
sunny day at **Haslemere Sun Club**

life to keep its naturist members happy. With an outdoor pool, two
miniten courts, a badminton court, boules terrain and table tennis,
there is plenty of opportunity for games and sports. A woodland
walk and the sauna suite offer alternative ways to relax.

The club house has full kitchen facilities for self catering, in
addition to barbeque facilities outside.

Visitors are welcome for day visits or camping.

Halcyon

Southsea, Hampshire

A weekday evening at this pool in Eastney gives naturists a
regular chance to swim without costumes. Visitors and potential
members are welcome to get in touch and arrange a visit.

Haslemere Sun Club

Headley Down, Hampshire

Haslemere Sun Club is a small family club in Hampshire not far
from the Surrey and Sussex borders. It is on a south-facing hill
in a peaceful pine wood setting.

Life revolves around the club's 18m by 6m pool which is heated
to an inviting 80F throughout the summer. Next to the pool is the

the UK's largest family naturist club in the south of England

Heritage

*enjoy a continental club in the UK
with large family membership,
close to the M4 and M3*

*heated openair pool
massive sunny conservatory
lots of camping and caravan pitches
lovely gardens and sunny lawns
open all year for members*

**Heath Ride
Crowthorne
BERKSHIRE
RG45 6BS**

tel: 01344 775 032
web: www.heritageclub.org

main lawn for sunbathing. The club has a well equipped pavilion with a kitchen where members can prepare their food.

There is a children's play area, barbecue, members' camping and chalets, and games courts. Although there are no holiday facilities, visitors are very welcome to arrange a weekend visit in advance.

Heritage Club

Crowthorne, Berkshire

Heritage's large family membership has spent many years improving the site into a welcoming and well-equipped naturist haven. Owned by the members, it is set in 5 acres of pine woodland bordering the Simons Wood National Trust site.

The club is open all year and its active season is from Easter to October when there may be several hundred on a sunny weekend enjoying the grounds. It's easy to reach from west London, sitting between the M3 and M4 south of Reading.

High on the list of attractions are the large heated swimming pool and new children's pool, complemented by a sauna and indoor and outdoor hot showers. Sports and leisure activities include a full-size tennis court, floodlit miniten courts, volleyball, shuffleboard and boules courts, table football and table tennis. The children's play areas include sand pits, climbing frames, swings and tree houses. Other facilities include the TV room, pavilion and BBQs, with planning permission granted for a new steam, sauna and Jacuzzi chalet. There are extensive lawns and gardens as well as secluded wooded areas and a large conservatory for greyer days.

Members and holiday visitors can use the 12 caravan pitches (no hook-up), numerous camping pitches and a mobile home. Prices and details are on the club website, along with booking forms.

Priority booking is given to existing family members at the

Heritage Club
The Secretary, Heritage club, Heath Ride, Crowthorne, Berkshire RG45 6BS
Tel: 01344 775032
Tel: 07799 777852
heritageclub@lycos.co.uk
www.heritageclub.org

Hundreds of naturists enjoy **Heritage**'s many attractions, which are open to members all year round. Picture supplied by the club

Invicta
The secretary, Invicta Sun Club, The Firs, Forge Lane, Sutton-by-Dover, Kent CT15 5DQ
Tel: 01622 762903
www.Invictasunclub.co.uk
InvictaSun@aol.com

Mill Bank
Tel: 01323 764426
millbanksecretary@btinternet.com

The Naturist Foundation
The Naturist Foundation (BB), Orpington, Kent BR5 4ET
Tel: 01689 871200
www.naturistfoundation.org
christine.ashford@ukonline.co.uk
natfound@ukonline.co.uk

Mill Bank, below, makes the most of its picturesque setting for naturist relaxation. The **Naturist Foundation**, pictured opposite above, has a huge site and draws naturist members from a large surrounding area; both pictures supplied by Shabden Leisure Circle, listed later in this section

start of the year, but after February all visitor booking requests are welcome. August bank holiday is reserved for members. All visitors need to contact the club in advance to make arrangements.

Invicta Sun Club
Between Dover and Deal, Kent
Invicta's naturist site extends over 4 acres of open woodland, set in a sheltered and secluded position amid farmland and trees. It prides itself on providing a safe, private venue for naturists to enjoy the sunshine and outdoors.

It has lawns for sunbathing, an outdoor swimming pool, courts for miniten, volleyball and badminton, and facilities for boules and table tennis. The large pavilion is open to all, with a gas ring for self-catering and tea making and a fireplace for colder weather. A canteen opens at weekends to provide coffee, tea and biscuits. There is a social and sports programme for members and visitors alike. Children have their own play chalet, adventure playground, swings and sand pit to keep them busy. The club has modern facilities, toilets and showers but no mains electricity.

There are tent and caravan sites available and three small self-catering cabins for hire. Members of other naturist clubs are very welcome to visit – prior booking must be made with the secretary. Membership enquiries are also welcome.

Mill Bank
Near Hastings, East Sussex
A picturesque site overlooking the beautiful Sussex countryside and English Channel is home to this friendly naturist club, which is run by its members.

It's within easy reach of naturist beaches at Fairlight and Norman's Bay, making it a convenient spot for naturists in the area. There is a club house and kitchen plus washing facilities. Members are looking for some land to offer camping and caravanning facilities. A barbeque on Saturday and Sunday evenings gives members and visitors a chance to meet and catch up.

Visitors and new members are made very welcome. Give the club a call to arrange a vist.

The Naturist Foundation
Orpington, Kent
It's the largest naturist site in the UK, and a uniquely convenient one at that. With just over 50 acres, the Naturist Foundation is the only naturist club inside the Greater London area. The woods and parkland are a paradise for naturists, a

The Naturist Foundation

All year round -
Boule, Miniten, Badminton etc Courts
Swimming pool (heated in Summer)
50acres of woodland & parkland
Full social & games programmes
Something for everyone

Orpington, BR5 4ET. - 01689 871200 - www.naturistfoundation.org

For Holidays -
Chalet (sleeps six)
Over 40 Tent/Caravan pitches
with electrical hook-ups
Easy access to Motorways
Ideal base for visiting London

haven from the stresses of life in the city and south-east England, and a mini nature reserve for native flora and fauna.

Unrivalled facilities are provided for several sports, particularly miniten, a form of short tennis popular among naturists throughout Britain. It's a naturist game in more ways than one: the foundation owns the copyright.

More than 100 seasonal campsites are available to the foundation's contributors, while visitors have the use of a camping meadow with 40 electrical hook-ups. There is also a fully furnished self-catering chalet to rent that sleeps up to six. A large pavilion is the hub for social activities during the main season of April to October. A canteen provides light meals and snacks at weekends and a wide choice of drinks is available from the adjacent licensed bar.

Founded as the North Kent Sun Club in 1948 on a much smaller site 5 miles away, the club moved to its present site in 1959. Among many other firsts, the Naturist Foundation is also Britain's only naturist recreational charity: in 1981 the founders gave the land to the charity to be used for naturism in perpetuity.

The Naturist Foundation has always prided itself on its comprehensive children's play facilities, which are constantly being updated. Special events for teenagers are organised by The Badgers and for young children by The Squirrels groups.

Whether you are just visiting on holiday, or looking for a regular naturist retreat, a warm welcome awaits you at the Naturist Foundation.

One of the peaceful chalets at the **Naturist Foundation**, below, and some of the many sporting facilities, bottom, including the organisation's own game of miniten. Images supplied by the foundation

Noah's Ark

Walton on Thames, Surrey
This naturist group holds swimming sessions on Sunday afternoons in the large local swimming pool. Contact the club if you're interested in joining or visiting.

Oxnat

Oxford, Oxfordshire
Founded in 1979, Oxnat members have bought 11 acres of woodland where they have developed a club house with sauna and lawns for sunbathing. The club holds a wide range of social and other events throughout the year.

Although the club's site lacks a swimming pool, members organise naturist swimming sessions at the local leisure centre in Didcot. The swims are held most weekends.

Reading Naturist Group

Reading, Berkshire
This friendly group of naked souls meets for a weekly swim in a local swimming baths, enjoying the pool without costumes on Thursday nights. With a 27-metre pool and hot showers, members come for the exercise, the naturism and the chance to catch up.

The group welcomes both experienced naturists and absolute first-timers alike. Contact the club first to arrange a visit.

Shabden Leisure Circle

Kent/East Sussex borders
Shabden is a non-profit naturist club which publishes the bi-monthly magazine *Naturist Life* and organises activities including leisure centre evenings, club and beach visits in the UK and abroad and get-togethers in members' homes. Details of all activities are published in *Naturist Life*.

Once a month Shabden hires the leisure centre at Marlie Farm, Dymchurch Road, New Romney (first

Noah's Ark
Tel: 01372 811655

Oxnat
www.oxnat.org.uk
oxnat@hotmail.com

Reading Naturist Group
Tel: 0118 942 0279
Tel: 0118 975 2202
www.rng.org.uk
enquiries@rng.org.uk

Shabden Leisure Circle
73 Williamson Road, Lydd on Sea,
Romney Marsh TN29 9NZ
Tel: 01797 364315
www.shabden.co.uk
editor@shabden.co.uk

Suzanne Piper of **Shabden Leisure Circle**, below, takes a dip at the Lydd on Sea address

Southampton Naturist Group
Tel: 023 8063 2199
c.mcdonald-martin@ntlworld.com

South Hants Country Club
Stockers, North Boarhunt, Fareham,
Hants PO17 6JS
Tel: 01329 832919
www.naturistholidays.co.uk
info@naturistholidays.co.uk

Wednesday) and Coghurst Hall, Ivyhouse Lane, Ore, near Hastings, East Sussex (fourth Monday). Both sites have a swimming pool, sauna and spa bath, and Coghurst also has fitness equipment.

The evenings run from 7.30pm to 9.30pm and cost £5.50 to non-members. Both events are open to all and visitors need to show a naturist card or ID.

At the club's Lydd on Sea address, which is home to the secretary, there is a small heated above-ground pool, a hot tub, a steam capsule, table tennis, fitness equipment, a barbecue and places to sunbathe. Dinner, bed and breakfast are available by prior arrangement as is aromatherapy massage. The club is affiliated to the Association of British Naturist Clubs.

Southampton Naturist Group

Bitterne, Hampshire
This naturist group hires out a local leisure centre for members and visitors to enjoy au naturel. The club meets weekly during autumn and winter, when the Bitterne leisure centre goes naturist for an hour every Sunday evening from 6.15pm to 7.15pm.

The club's meetings take place from the last Sunday in September to the last Sunday before Easter. There are a swimming pool and flume for visitors to enjoy. Contact the club for more information.

South Hants Country Club

Near Fareham, Hampshire
South Hants Country Club is set in a small valley in 11 acres of Hampshire's beautiful countryside. The attractively landscaped grounds are south-facing with extensive sunbathing lawns, beyond which are the games courts and children's play area.

The indoor leisure complex, complete with indoor pool, sauna, steam room and whirlpool spa, is situated at the centre of the grounds adjoining the bar and restaurant which overlook the heated 60-foot outdoor swimming pool and terrace.

For the energetic naturist there is a volleyball court, three miniten (short tennis) courts, a boules terrain and table tennis.

The club is a particularly popular holiday destination, having received a glowing write-up in the *Sunday Times* and holding four stars from the English Tourism Council. Accommodation is available in holiday caravans with one or two bedrooms, lounge

South Hants, pictured opposite, has been praised as a classic British naturist club with up-to-date facilities

Luxury holiday homes for sale at South Hants Country Club

*We have an exciting selection of new and used holiday homes for sale,
all fully furnished and connected to main services. Prices start at around £12000*

*You are free to stay in your holiday home as often or as long as you wish between March and October,
all summer if you choose, plus long weekends in the winter.*

*We offer excellent amenities including Indoor and Outdoor Swimming Pools, Sauna, Steam room and Whirlpool spa,
a Restaurant and Bar where you can dine out and make new friends, plus many other sports and leisure facilities.*

*If you would like to know more why not arrange to spend a day with us, view the
holiday homes and enjoy the use of our leisure facilities free of charge.*

**Contact Michael Wilson at South Hants Country Club
North Boarhunt, Fareham, Hampshire, PO17 6JS
Tel: 01329 832919   Fax: 01329 834506   Email: info@naturistholidays.co.uk**

diner, full kitchen, shower and toilet. Bookings can be for weeks or short breaks in the summer and weekends in winter. Visitors with tents and touring caravans are welcome from Easter to October. Electric hook-ups available.

South Hants also has club members, many of whom have their own holiday homes situated in the club grounds. New members are also always welcome, though the club is couples and families only.

There are usually new, and sometimes used, holiday homes for sale if you want a place to call your own in this naturist haven.

Surrey Downs Sun Club

Between Guildford, Dorking and Woking, Surrey
A secluded hillside, surrounded by woodland and overlooking the Surrey downs, is just the sort of place to enjoy naturism. And since 1941 members have been doing just that, developing the site as a family and social club.

As the club itself says, the ethos is "for all members to enjoy themselves whilst contributing to the well-being and happiness of others".

The grounds include a clubhouse, chalets, children's play area and a solar-panel heated pool which is open from May to September. There are two miniten/badminton courts and a boules court and a number of lawns with a convenient mix of sun and shade.

The large clubhouse has a comfortable lounge and function area with a fully fitted communal kitchen. There is also a 12 - seat sauna and shower area.

The club welcomes genuine naturists as day or holiday visitors. It has camping and overnight facilities but no site warden so arrangements need to be made in advance.

Valerian Sun Club

Havenstreet, Isle of Wight
Valerian is a member-owned club with 6 acres of woodland. Around 60 members share this peaceful site with a wide variety of birds and wildlife, and there

Surrey Downs Sun Club
PO Box 75, Woking, Surrey GU22 7XB
Tel: 0786 787 4510
www.sdsc.org.uk
membership@sdsc.org.uk

Valerian Sun Club
Walkers Hill Copse, Havenstreet, Isle of Wight PO33 4DT
Tel: 07931 281360
www.valerian.fsworld.co.uk
valeriansunclub@hotmail.com
valerianholidays@hotmail.com

South Hants, pictured opposite top and middle, offers four-star holiday accommodation. **Surrey Downs,** pictured opposite bottom and below, is a tranquil naturist club near Guildford with plenty of space for cheerful socialising and relaxation

The White House Members Club
PO Box 1026, Warlingham,
Surrey CR6 9FJ
Tel: 07952 788377
www.whitehouseclub.org.uk
info@whitehouseclub.org.uk

are places to sit surrounded by the woodland or next to the pond area.

The club house has a kitchen and other facilities while outside there is a boules court, barbeque and children's play area. Holidaymakers enjoying a trip to the Isle of Wight and its naturist beaches (see Beaches section) can camp at the club, hire the club caravan, or simply visit for the day – prior notice must be given before any visit.

The White House

Near Caterham, Surrey

"If you've ever felt the need to unwind, to put aside the hassles of life and luxuriate in a bit of calm free time, you're a naturist at heart," says the White House. And with London on its doorstep, the club has plenty of members who welcome the leafy seclusion of its 5 acres.

Skinny-dipping in the 50-foot pool is one major reason to join the club. It's open all year and is just a few yards' dash from the spacious sauna. Other sports include two tennis courts, indoor and outdoor table tennis, an exercise room, a badminton court, basketball hoop, a volleyball area and a picturesque boules court. There is a large children's play area too.

The club house, a substantial brick building which gives the club its name, has 10 bedrooms for hire, a licensed bar by the sunny patio area and a kitchen for members to use. There is a TV room, a children's playroom, several barbeques and a huge conservatory. Founded in 1933, it is one of the UK's oldest clubs and a welcoming family atmosphere has developed over the decades with a busy social calendar for those interested.

Among the many reasons to join the **White House** are its 50-foot pool, beautiful hillside setting, plentiful sports facilities and friendly members, pictured below and opposite

Members are particularly proud of the beautiful terraced grounds, planted with trees, shrubs, flowers and plenty of secluded lawns for reading and sunbathing. An article in *The Express* newspaper in 2004 commented favourably on the beautifully landscaped gardens and genuine naturist atmosphere.

The club welcomes prospective new members, and is easily reached from much of London by train or car. Contact the club first to fix up a preliminary visit.

Eastern

Arcadians of Greenglades

Near Billericay, Essex

Set in 4.5 acres of peaceful Essex woodland, Arcadians describes itseslf as the club where you can shed your worries with your clothes. It is a family club, owned and cared for by the members.

It has an active social calendar including (not too serious) sports competitions, sports just for fun, and "plenty of space to just chill out".

Among the attractions are lawns for sunbathing, an outdoor pool and a sauna. Activities include a children's play area, a miniten court, a badminton court, four boules terrains and table tennis.

There is also a club room, a pavilion, a fully equipped kitchen, barbeques and tea on Sunday afternoons. Members can pitch tents to stay overnight.

A variety of evening socials are held throughout the year. The club also hosts monthly winter swim, sauna, steam and spa evenings at a sports centre in nearby Billericay, which run from October to April.

Although lacking the resources to entertain casual visitors, Arcadians welcomes membership enquiries and prides itself on welcoming newcomers.

"After a few days at Greenglades you feel like you have belonged for years in our little piece of heaven on earth," as the club puts it.

Arcadians
Tel: 07813 346631
arcadians@msn.com

A warm welcome awaits bare souls at the charming **Cambridge Outdoor Club**, opposite. And the tranquil grounds of **Arcadians**, below, are a naturist haven owned and cared for by the members. Picture opposite by Mick Goody, pictures below supplied by Arcadians

Blackthorns

Sharnbrook, near Bedford, Bedfordshire

With more than 200 members, Blackthorns says it has created the perfect place to relax and enjoy the wooded Bedfordshire countryside. Over 35 years of care have gone into developing the 15-acre site, with quiet woodland walks making the most of its natural setting.

Facilities include an outdoor pool, showers, two miniten courts, four petanque pistes, volleyball, a children's play area, a badminton court and a crazy golf course. It has both a general pavilion and a children's pavilion, and barbeque facilities.

Holiday visitors are welcome at weekends but need to be members of British Naturism and bring their cards (see page 6). Tents, caravans and motorhomes are all accepted. The club also has an active social and sporting calendar throughout the year.

Broadlands Sun Association

Five miles south of Norwich, Norfolk

Set in 24 acres of woodland, Broadlands describes itself as the ideal holiday venue for all the family. There is much at the club and nearby to attract holidaymakers to the area.

Blackthorns
Tel: 01234 782212
www.blackthorns.org.uk
enquiry@blackthorns.org.uk

Broadlands
Brickle Road, Stoke Holy Cross,
Norwich NR14 8NG
Tel: 01508 492907
www.paston.co.uk/broadlands
broadlands@paston.co.uk

Blackthorns (facing page top and middle left) has an active social and sporting life, while **Broadlands** (facing page middle right and bottom) has much to attract the holiday naturist. Middle two pictures by Steve Thompson; others supplied by the clubs

BROADLANDS

Rain or shine — the place in the country for all the family

Indoor swimming pool	**Fully serviced caravans**
Sun lounge	**Modern campsite**
Club house	**Facilities for disabled**
Sports	**Bistro**

For details write or telephone
Broadland Sun Association Ltd, Brickle Road, Stoke Holy Cross, Norwich NR14 8NG
Tel: 01508 492907
www.paston.co.uk/broadlands

Cambridge Outdoor Club
The Orchard, The Borough, Aldreth,
Cambridgeshire CB6 3PJ
Tel: 01353 741335
www.cambridgeoutdoor.org
arprinters@aol.com

Cambridge Outdoor Club is proud
of its welcoming and attractive
grounds. Picture below Rod Currie,
pictures bottom Mick Goody

The club is a short drive from the coast and many sandy beaches, including some naturist beaches. It is also close to the medieval city of Norwich and the Norfolk Broads.

It was voted the British Naturism club of the year in 2004 and aims to attract both members and holiday visitors alike. The club has an indoor swimming pool, a sun lounge, sauna, children's play area, miniten courts, badminton, petanque, volleyball, table tennis and short-mat bowls. For a back to nature experience you can go skinny-dipping in the natural lake, or try your hand at fishing.

There are fully serviced caravans for hire, sites for touring caravans and tents and hook-ups for electricity. There are also modern showers, toilets and a laundry room. The club has full facilities for disabled visitors and, unusually for a naturist club, a resident warden. For cooler days and nights there is a heated clubhouse with TV room. Visitors are very welcome with advance notice, and membership enquiries are always invited.

Cambridge Outdoor Club

Ely, Cambridgeshire
The Cambridge Outdoor Club is one of the oldest and arguably the prettiest club in Cambridgeshire, tucked away in the heart of

the countryside between Cambridge and Ely. The members of this family-orientated club are proud of their small but well-maintained haven, with its comfortable clubhouse, open-air pool, sauna, sun lawns, children's play area, petanque and miniten courts. The club is busiest during the summer, but is open to members all year and there is an active winter social programme.

If you just want to visit or stay for a short holiday, the club welcomes holidaymakers with BN or INF membership cards (see page 6 for joining details). Tents, touring caravans and campervans are all welcome for short stays, but pitches have no mains electricity points and can not accommodate van awnings.

Potential visitors need to make arrangements before turning up as the club has limited space.

As for potential members, the club welcomes all membership enquiries, and says it would particularly suit couples and families living or working around Silicon Fen. The club maintains a balance of single members as a percentage of overall membership, which changes from season to season.

Cinema in the Buff

Cambridgeshire

This innovative group of cinema-goers has found a way to stay naturist all year round. As the name suggests, the group meets regularly to watch a current box office film au naturel.

However, there's more to the club than simply watching films: it has a strong social side and attracts people from all over the country. After the film members gather in the foyer/bar for a light meal and screening of an older naturist film.

Originally based in The Grand Venue, an art deco cinema in Ramsey, Cambridgeshire, the 'Buffs welcome all naturists to join them.

Croft Country Club

Between Wisbech, Cambs, and Downham Market, Norfolk

Croft is at the heart of the unique fens region, on the Norfolk/Cambridgeshire border near Three Holes village. Among the many facilities in its 12 acres are four tree-screened meadows with superb gardens, a riverside dog walk and plenty of space for relaxed sunbathing.

The managers Dave and Celia run a full social

Cinema in the Buff
Tel: 07952 680091
Tel: 07745 333314
mark@citb.wanadoo.co.uk

Croft Country Club
Dave and Celia Underwood, Croft Country Club, Toll Road, Three Holes, Wisbech, Cambridgeshire PE14 9JD
Tel: 01354 638445
www.croftcountryclub.co.uk
bookings@croftcountryclub.co.uk

Cinema in the Buff has a friendly social side to its movie-watching, with naturists meeting to chat before and after the screenings.
Picture by Mark Yates

Cinema in the Buff

Far East Naturist Swim
Tel: 01502 512497

Meadowlands
Tel: 01473 726037
www.meadowlandsleisureclub.co.uk
Enquire@meadowlandsleisureclub.co.uk

calendar in a relaxed atmosphere, with theme nights once a month. There is a huge choice of activities on site, including a large outdoor heated pool, a luxury hydro spa pool and steam room (pay), volleyball, miniten, petanque, shuffleboard, an 18-hole putting green, lawn bowls, clay pigeon shooting and archery.

Croft has a newly enlarged clubhouse with log fire, modern kitchen, games room with pool table and TV, a sauna (pay), a hot tub (pay) and an adjoining barbeque area and children's playhouse. Indoor facilities include short-mat bowls, table tennis and a music centre.

The club welcomes holidaymakers, with 75 electric hook-ups for caravans, motorhomes and tents. It also hires out caravans and in a recent innovation has started offering the chance to buy your very own new log cabins at the club. Call or see Croft's website for more details.

Visitor facilities include three washroom/shower/toilet blocks plus laundry facilities (pay). Contact the club in advance if you want to visit, book a holiday or ask about membership.

Far East Naturist Swim (Fens)

Diss, Norfolk
Fens says it is "for when you've nothing on", which is the best way to enjoy the swimming, sauna, steam and spa at Diss with this friendly naturist group.

With regular sessions from September to May, the club's activities are based around the 25-metre pool. A learner pool, sauna, steam room and spa are also available for naturist use.

The club prides itself on keeping its fees low and all members are encouraged to join British Naturism (see page 6).

Croft Country Club's large outdoor pool is a popular attraction, available to both members and holidaymakers alike. Picture by Charlie Simonds of Parafotos (www.parafotos.co.uk)

Meadowlands Leisure Club

Ipswich, Suffolk
This naturist club meets in a small privately owned site to enjoy swimming, boules and of course naturist sunbathing.

The club also has a clubhouse, with a kitchen and barbeque facilities on offer. Members also organise social events in the club and further afield. Contact the club for more information about a visit or membership.

Merryhill Leisure

Near Norwich, Norfolk

Merryhill is a vibrant club which attracts both local naturists and holidaymakers with its fine facilities, handy location and peaceful woodland setting.

It has an excellent heated outdoor pool open from late May to mid September, and in the winter a heated indoor pool open on Saturday lunchtime, Sunday lunchtime and Sunday night. Activities continue out of the water with two floodlit miniten courts, petanque, volleyball and badminton. Children have their own play area, while indoor facilities include the sauna and heated clubhouse with table tennis, darts and pool table.

Set on a gentle grassy slope amid mature pines and mixed woodlands, Merryhill enjoys relaxing views and has acres of fine woodland walks on its doorstep. The area is also popular for cycling trips.

The club welcomes tourists using it as their naturist holiday base. Just 8 miles away, Norwich has great shopping, historical sites, museums and countless pubs. Merryhill is also well placed for visiting the Broads and the Norfolk coast.

There is a large camping area with 10-amp electric hook-ups,

Merryhill Leisure
Telegraph Hill, Honingham, Norwich
NR9 5AT
Tel: 01603 881411
www.merryhillleisure.co.uk
info@merryhillleisure.co.uk

A vibrant club with a busy social side, **Merryhill** encourages tourists to use the club as a holiday base; picture below Steve Thompson. Bottom: the men get stuck into a game of miniten, a form of short tennis popular among naturists; picture by Charlie Simonds (www.parafotos.co.uk)

MERRYHILL LEISURE
the friendly naturist club

Set in 16 acres of beautiful parkland with a natural and tranquil setting

• Heated clubhouse • Table tennis
• 2 Floodlit miniten courts • Darts
• Large pool table • Volleyball court
• Petanque lanes • Communal BBQ
• Heated showers and sauna
• Washing and drying facilities
• Superb heated outdoor pool (open in season) • Use of heated indoor pool Saturdays and Sundays
• Merryhill has a reputation of having some of the best dances, with top acts • Discos • Fancy Dress night

Also – Why not own your own holiday home at Merryhill? New and used holiday homes for sale on site.

For more information send 1st class stamp to:
**Merryhill Leisure, Telegraph Hill,
Honingham, Norwich NR9 5AT
or Tel: 01603 881411
E-mail: info@merryhillleisure.co.uk
Why not visit our web site: www.merryhillleisure.co.uk**

Also available – Touring caravan and tent pitches with or without electric hook-ups. Fully serviced holiday caravan for hire with WC, shower, TV and fridge (your home away from home).

C.C.B.N

and camping vans on site to hire. It has all amenities, including heated shower room, kitchen/laundry room and a chemical toilet disposal area. It is a Calor gas stockist.

Day visitors are also welcome; all visitors should call the club in advance.

Mildenhall Naturist Swimming Club

Mildenhall and Newmarket, Suffolk

This group has found its naturist swims so popular it has had to expand to a second venue in Newmarket. A positive and open attitude to publicity has attracted very favourable comment from local newspapers and radio, bringing new members and greater public support.

As the *Cambridge Evening News* put it in 2005: "They harm no one, and people participate for sociable reasons. Good luck to all those who decide to get their kit off and take the plunge."

The group plans to continue its monthly swim and sauna in Mildenhall's local authority pool, with a monthly swim in Newmarket also planned from September to April. Contact the club or look at the website for latest details.

Visitors are welcome but should check the club's entry requirements on the website or by phone.

Oakwood Sun Club

Romford, Essex

Owned by its members, Oakwood has 6 acres of mixed woodland conveniently sited between Romford and Brentwood.

There is an outdoor heated pool, miniten, boules and volleyball courts, with a clubhouse for socialising throughout the year.

Visitors are welcome and should contact the club in advance.

Pevors Farm Cottages

Essex/Suffolk borders

A unique naturist holiday haven, Pevors Farm is widely admired for its top-quality facilities and accommodation. Set in a 400-acre arable farm, the site has four self-catering cottages converted from 18th-century farm buildings. The cottages have all the modern facilities you could expect, earning them a four-star rating from the English Tourism Council.

The site is a holiday resort rather than a club, and was opened by its naturist owners John and Margaret in November 2002.

Mildenhall Naturist SC
Tel: 07946 886843
http://mildenhall.naturism.org.uk
mildenhall@naturism.org.uk

Oakwood Sun Club
Tel: 07960 109041
www.oakwoodsun.co.uk
oakwoodsun@hotmail.com

Pevors Farm Cottages
Pevors Farm Cottages, Southey Green, Sible Hedingham, Essex CO9 3RN
Tel: 01787 460830
www.pevorsfarm.co.uk
naturist@pevorsfarm.co.uk

All sorts of sports are on offer at **Merryhill**, including boules, opposite above. Picture by Charlie Simonds of Parafotos (www.parafotos.co.uk)

AWARD WINNING
Unique Naturist Retreat
on the Essex / Suffolk Border

Four individual cottage conversions from traditional 18th Century farm buildings. Heated indoor pool and south facing courtyards and sun-bathing lawns. Situated on a 400 acre farm with woodland, lakes and meadows.

For our brochure, please contact Margaret and John Lewis on

01787 460 830
www.pevorsfarm.co.uk
E-mail: naturist@pevorsfarm.co.uk

Pevors Farm Cottages

English Tourism Council

★★★★ SELF-CATERING

Welcome HOST

Facilities include a leisure room, sunroom and 40-foot by 10-foot indoor heated pool, all grouped around two courtyards.

Guests can enjoy back-to-nature walks along footpaths surrounded by birds and butterflies, sit by the carp pools or take a longer walk to a bluebell wood, an ideal spot for picnics. It's all naturist and there are plenty of areas for sunbathing in natural seclusion.

The surrounding region has picturesque villages to explore and is the driest part of the UK.

The owners welcome naturist holidaymakers, and have been given awards by both British Naturism and Parafotos, the naturist production company.

Pevors Farm is a top-rated naturist holiday centre, much praised by visitors. Picture opposite top supplied by Shabden Leisure Circle, all other pictures by Charlie Simonds of Parafotos (www.parafotos.co.uk)

Bare bathers swim in formation at **Prested Hall** during a fundraising event for Essex Air Ambulance, which the club members actively support

Prested Hall
www.prested.com/natswim.htm

Club Soleil
Tel: 01733 562294
Tel: 07890 105346
www.soleil.f9.co.uk
june@soleil.f9.co.uk

Spielplatz
Tel: 01923 672126
www.spielplatzoasis.co.uk
info@spielplatzoasis.co.uk

Prested Hall

Kelvedon, near Colchester, Essex
Three local naturist clubs organise this popular swim on the second and fourth Saturdays of the month, from 6.30pm-10pm, plus some Friday evenings clothing-optional sessions. Club members and non-members alike are welcome to attend; contact the club to arrange your first visit.

Club Soleil

Peterborough, Cambridgeshire
Established in July 1996, Club Soleil is a family-orientated naturist swim club based in Peterborough. With an open "if you're a naturist – you're welcome" policy, the club says it has a reputation for its friendliness and visitors are assured a warm welcome.

The club organises naturist events at various locations in East Anglia and the Midlands. Full details of the events and facilities are published on the club website. All venues are suitable for disabled visitors.

Club Soleil does not have its own grounds but organises social events in the summer and exchange visits with other swim clubs and landed clubs in East Anglia and the Midlands.

Visitors are welcome at all events, and after three visits asks you to apply for membership.

Spielplatz

St Albans, Hertfordshire
"Naturism has so much to offer as a form of recreation, perhaps now more than ever before," is Spielplatz's shrewd observation on a lifestyle it knows better than most. "With our busy and stressful lifestyles it is enjoyable and healthy to be able to relax in peaceful surroundings. The trappings and fashions of the 21st century recede."

The club's commitment to the ideals of naturism are deeply rooted and go back a long way. It was one of the very first places in Britain to become a naturist club, its name redolent of 1930s German naturist pioneers.

If you want to understand the thinking that underpins the modern naturist movement, Spielplatz sums it up thus:
● Promotes physical and mental health
● Is socially constructive
● Is consistent with equality
● Encourages cohesive families
● Is more comfortable than clothing
● Does not discriminate

Spielplatz invites others to enjoy the pleasures of social nudity. It has a children's play area that will keep the more boisterous ones occupied. For older children (of all ages) there is a recently refurbished heated outdoor swimming pool, courts for boules, badminton, volleyball and miniten.

The most popular activity is sunbathing, whether in direct sun or in the comfort of the shade of the club's mature trees. The lawn at the front of the clubhouse is the ideal place for eating al fresco and truly au naturel.

Spielplatz, below, holds a special place in the hearts of British naturists, marking 75 years of clothes-free leisure in 2005. Pictures supplied by Mark Yates

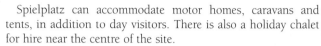

Springwood Sun Club
The secretary, Springwood Sun Club,
Cooks Hall Road, West Bergholt,
Colchester, Essex CO6 3EY
Tel: 07789 044072
www.springwood.org.uk
springwoodclub@hotmail.com

Springwood, below, mixes natural
woodland with modern facilities for
its naturist haven. Picture supplied by
the club

Spielplatz can accommodate motor homes, caravans and tents, in addition to day visitors. There is also a holiday chalet for hire near the centre of the site.

The clubhouse includes a 20-person sauna, pool and table tennis tables and a south-facing solarium designed for comfort and warmth.

Springwood Sun Club

Colchester, Essex

True to its name, this 6-acre club has both a spring and a wood. It is set in ancient woodland, with a spring-fed lake adding natural beauty to the naturist experience. Yellow water irises flower to mark the start of the season, while water lilies bloom over the summer.

Run by its members, Springwood has plenty of modern facilities set among the natural environment to keep its members and visitors happy. The new pavilion features a kitchen and TV room and the club room has a woodburning fireplace to warm the evening gatherings. A covered barbeque area completes the built facilities.

In the beautiful grounds, an outdoor swimming pool, two miniten courts, three petanque courts, a children's play area and a volleyball court keep members active. And of course there are lawns for those who simply want to lie in the sun and relax.

Tents and motor homes can be brought to the site but it is unsuitable for caravans. Visitors are made very welcome and should contact the club in advance.

Sun-Folk Society

St Albans, Hertfordshire

A friendly atmosphere, beautiful grounds and excellent facilities have been attracting naturists to Sun-Folk since 1931. Lawns for sunbathing are sheltered by the natural woodland surrounding the site. Set in 5 acres, the club's facilities include an outdoor pool, miniten, badminton and volleyball courts, a petanque pitch, children's play area and a sauna. The members organise social events throughout the year, with a large clubhouse and members' kitchen providing the venue.

The club has a camping area for members. Visitors are always made welcome; contact the secretary to make arrangements first.

Watford Naturist Swimming Club

Watford and St Albans, Hertfordshire

With 230 members, WNSC is a popular naturist swimming club handy for Hertfordshire and much of London. It holds two regular events: a swim each Friday in Watford, and a bi-monthly Saturday night leisure centre swim in St Albans. Both events are ideal for newcomers to naturism.

The club is proud of its sporting prowess, although it stresses that swimmers of all abilities are welcome. For those interested it has a first-rate swimming team, which won the national British Naturism swimming gala top club trophy in 2003 and 2004.

As well as swimming, club members also participate in other naturist sports, such as running, petanque, badminton and miniten. The social side of the club is strong, with members adjourning to a bar at a local naturist club after the weekly swims, and an annual dinner.

At Watford the club uses a 33-yard pool. At St Albans there is a 33-metre main pool, children's pool, inflatable treasure island, two flumes, diving boards, health suite with sauna, steam room and spa bath plus a café serving hot and cold food and drinks. All facilities are naturist for the night.

The club welcomes visitors. Bring a form of ID – either a British Naturism or other naturist club card (see page 6), or driving licence or similar.

Sun-Folk Society
The secretary, The Sun-Folk Society, Hazel Road, Park St, St Albans, Herts AL2 2AJ
Tel: 01727 873576 (Sundays)
Tel: 01582 614086 (Evenings and Saturdays)
www.sun-folk.org.uk
info@sun-folk.org.uk

Watford NSC
Tel: 01923 219220 (Recorded message with details of events)
www.wnsc.org.uk
info@wnsc.org.uk

Naturists in the Watford and St Albans area are keen users of the 33-yard pool in Watford, below. Picture supplied by **Watford Naturist Swimming Club**

East and West Midlands

Avon Outdoor Club

Stratford-upon-Avon, Warwickshire
This small, family club has a south-facing woodland setting and a range of facilities including a pool and children's play area in its 2.5 acres.

Visitors are welcome and should contact the club in advance.

Bare With Me

Newcastle-under-Lyme, Staffordshire
This group of naturists meets regularly in the Jubilee Pools in Newcastle-under-Lyme for an evening of swimming and enjoying the facilities.

With a full-size pool, flume, sauna and Turkish suite plus a large relaxation area, there is plenty to help you keep fit or unwind as you choose.

If you want to bare with Bare With Me, contact the club first for more details.

Charnwood Acres Country Club

Ratby, Leicestershire
A large club within very easy reach of the M1 (junction 22), Charnwood has 17 acres of meadow and woodland with scenic walks and plenty of facilities. The club is privately owned and open all year.

Handy for Nottingham, Derby and Leicester, naturists come to enjoy the outdoor heated pool (in season), and play games on the miniten, petanque, shuffleboard and volleyball courts. Woodland walks and a children's play area complete the outdoor facilities.

Indoors there is a large clubhouse with pool table, table tennis, darts and a licensed bar. Snacks and bar meals are on offer during the season.

Holidaymakers can use the pitches and electrical hook-ups for caravans or tents, and there is one caravan on site to rent. Visitors are welcome to get in touch.

Desford Swim

Desford, Leicestershire
This swimming club meets weekly for naturist bathing, table tennis and badminton at a local pool.

Contact the club for details about organising a visit.

Avon Outdoor Club
The secretary, 3 Manor Avenue, Great Wyrley, Staffordshire WS6 6NS.
Tel: 01922 416670

BWM
Tel: 01782 281189
Tel: 07971 050661

Charnwood Acres
Charnwood Acres Country Club, Markfield Road, Ratby, Leicestershire LE6 0LU
Tel: 01530 243958

Desford Swim
Tel: 0116 287 1008

Nottingham Sun Club, pictured opposite by Steve Thompson, is one of the Midlands' long-established naturist sites

East Midland Sunfolk
The secretary, East Midland Sunfolk,
Laughterton, Lincolnshire LN1 2JT
Tel: 07734 882 333

Swans
Tel: 07811 451545
swimswans@hotmail.com

Tess Swimming Club
Tel: 0775 127 6755

Northampton Sun Group
PO Box 7234, Market Harborough
LE16 7YZ
Tel: 08707 650558
www.northamptonsungroup.org.uk

East Midland Sunfolk

Near Gainsborough and Lincoln, Lincolnshire
One of Britain's early pioneers in the naturist movement Percy Walford went on to found this club in 1947. The 8 acres of grounds have matured into a landscape designed around naturist relaxation.

There is a heated outdoor pool, and sports areas including four miniten courts, a petanque court and a bowling room. The clubhouse has a kitchen and other facilities. Children have both a play area and a club room with TV and pool table.

The site has a licence for 110 caravans and the club can accommodate visiting caravans and motorhomes. All visitors are welcome and should contact the club in advance.

Swans

Erdington swimming pool, Birmingham
The name stands for steam, water and naturist sauna – all of which are available at the club's monthly meetings. The club uses the same facilities as the Tess swimming club (see details listed below), including the pool, sauna, steam and Turkish lounge area.

Visitors are always welcome and must contact the club in advance.

Tess Swimming Club

Erdington swimming pool, Birmingham
This naturist members' club meets for swimming sessions at the Erdington swimming pool in Birmingham on Thursdays from 8.30pm-10.00pm (doors close 8.45pm).

Facilities include the full-size pool, sauna, two steam rooms, plunge pool and Turkish suite. Visitors are welcome, preferably with a naturist membership card from British Naturism/INF, but must contact the club first before turning up. See page 6 for details on BN/INF membership.

Northampton Sun Group

Northampton, Northamptonshire
This club makes regular use of an indoor leisure centre for naturist swimming and socialising.

The centre has two pools, plus a health suite including sauna and steam room and a gym.

As the club says, if you share the view that you don't need to be clothed to enjoy swimming, sun and saunas, it may be for you. To arrange a visit, contact the club in advance.

Nottingham Sun Club

Near Hucknall, Nottinghamshire

Nottingham Sun Club is a long-established naturist venue set in a quiet location, with well-maintained grounds and excellent facilities. Its 5 acres of land are owned and cared for by the members.

The site provides open spaces for sunbathing, with natural seclusion from the extensive rhododendron hedging around the edges. In the spring the flowering rhododendrons are a magnificent sight for any nature lover, as are the mature trees and varied wildlife.

The site houses 43 chalets, owned by individual members, and a members' campsite. A smaller campsite has pitches for visitors.

A comprehensive programme of social events takes place throughout the year and the club boasts its own expert DJ, who entertains into the early hours on function nights.

Sports facilities are free to all, on a casual basis or in group tournaments. Among the options are a covered heated swimming pool, three miniten courts, a volleyball court, a children's play area and covered sand pit, a boules court, a tennis court and a badminton court.

In the club's two pavilions are kitchens and other facilities, a table tennis table, a pool table and a tuck shop for sweets, ice cream, soft drinks and so on.

Nottingham Sun Club
The membership secretary, NSC, PO Box 5027, Hucknall, Nottinghamshire NG15 6UE
Tel: 07977 490428
www.nottinghamsunclub.co.uk

Nottingham Sun Club's many activities, below, pictured by BN photographer Steve Thompson

Oaklands Sun Club
The secretary, PO Box 5544, Sileby,
Loughborough LE12 7WS
marie_bailey@hotmail.com

Spectrum
PO Box 3274, Shirley, Solihull B90 4WH
Tel: 07771 653709
www.spectrumclub.pwp.blueyonder.co.uk
spectrum@tesco.net

Sungrove
Prospect Lane, Waltham Rd, Brigsley,
Grimsby, Lincolnshire DN37 0RQ
Tel: 07745 106008
Tel: 01472 233712

Sungrove naturist club is surrounded by trees for seclusion and undisturbed relaxation

Additional facilities for which a small charge is made are the sauna, hot tub and showers.

Campsites are available to holidaymakers (bring your own equipment) for tents and motorhomes. Electric hook-ups have been planned for these sites.

All members of British Naturism or members of other naturist clubs are welcome.

Membership is open to families, couples and singles. Contact the club for more information.

Oaklands Sun Club
Leicester, Leicestershire
Oaklands members have developed a full range of facilities in their 7-acre family naturist club.

There is a heated swimming pool, games courts and lawn for sunbathing. Indoors, the large clubhouse has a kitchen for self-catering and a sauna and showers.

Visitors should contact the club first to make arrangements.

Spectrum
South Birmingham
This naturist swimming club meets on Saturdays at the Northfield Baths in Bristol Road, Birmingham, to use the pool, gym, sauna and steam room.

Spectrum aims to create a relaxed and friendly environment for naturists to enjoy swimming and socialising.

If you're interesting in a regular bare bathing opportunity, contact the club in advance to arrange a visit.

Sungrove
Near Grimsby, Lincolnshire
This naturist club is owned and looked after by its members. Surrounded by trees, it provides a peaceful place to enjoy sunbathing, swimming in the pool and the sauna.

There are courts for miniten and petanque, and a clubhouse with cooking facilities for members to use. The club has five spaces for caravans or campervans and some sites for tents.

Visitors are welcome, with a small charge to pay. Contact the club to arrange a visit or enquire about membership.

Telford Naturist Club

Two miles from Telford, Shropshire
Telford Naturist Club is a large members' club, situated in 25 acres of woodland, with around 230 members. It prides itself on excellent facilities, a reputation for friendliness and an active and diverse social life.

Among the many attractions are the outdoor heated pool, sauna and showers. There is a licensed bar in the large clubhouse, and active members can choose from volleyball, miniten, boules and shuffleboard courts, a children's play area and room and acres of woodland walks.

Naturist holiday visitors are accommodated on 13 caravan, tent or motor home pitches with electric hook-ups. It welcomes all British Naturism, INF and other genuine naturist club members as visitors.

If you'd like to visit or ask about joining, contact the club first.

Telford Naturist Club
TNC Ltd, The Windings, Grange Lane, Redhill, Telford, Shropshire TF2 9PB
Tel: 01952 610873

There is plenty of green space at **Telford Naturist Club**, pictured below, with an old minehead providing vivid contrast. Picture below left supplied by the club, below right by Roger Hart

Yorkshire

Ashdene Sun Club

Elland, West Yorkshire
Ashdene describes itself as a natural haven for both wildlife and naturists, in the heart of West Yorkshire. Members have an active social life at the club with theme nights and occasional shows.

Sports facilities include miniten and boules, with a sauna, patio, lawns and barbeque area for more leisurely pursuits. The club also has a bar.

Visitors are very welcome and there are several pitches for visitors' caravans, mostly with hook-ups, plus a camping area for tents. There are also two club caravans for hire.

Leeds Naturist Group

Leeds and local area, West Yorkshire
Much more than just a swimming club, the Leeds Naturist Group has been organising activities in the area since 1985. The club's main fixture is a weekly naturist session at a leisure centre in the city, with a pool, spa pool and steam room on offer to participants.

Other events include social gatherings, an annual picnic on a naturist beach, and events held at other naturist clubs around the region.

Visitors and locals are welcome and should contact the club for more details; the club sends out information by post so remember to include your address.

Pendale Sun Club

Brighouse, West Yorkshire
Pendale has been a naturist club for more than 50 years and reckons it has the smallest grounds of any UK naturist club. However in less than 1 acre the members have fitted in a clubhouse with kitchen, sunbathing lawns, a children's play area, volleyball and a boules area.

Day visitors are welcome and should contact the club in advance.

Ashdene Sun Club
The secretary, Ashdene, 500 Elland Road, Elland, West Yorkshire HX5 9JB
Tel: 01422 379500
www.ashdene.net

Leeds Naturist Group
The secretary, LNG, PO Box 675, Bradford BD2 3UH
Tel: 0113 287 3616
leeds_naturists@yahoo.co.uk

Pendale Sun Club
The secretary, Pendale SC, PO Box 4, Brighouse, West Yorkshire HD6 1DE
pendalesc@yahoo.com

Indoors and out, naturists doing what feels natural; picture opposite top by John Hale, submitted by John Paine, opposite bottom by Charlie Simonds (www.parafotos.co.uk). Below the **Leeds Naturist Group** enjoying their weekly swim; picture supplied by the club

Ryedale Naturist Club
The Old Pipe House, 1 Victoria Road,
Malton, North Yorkshire YO17 7JJ
Tel: 01653 697823
Tel: 01904 708123
Tel: 01430 861224

South Yorkshire Sun Club
Tel: 01427 728494
Tel: 01302 770861

Valley Club
Tel: 0113 250 3336 (daytime)
Tel: 0113 258 8705 (evenings)
http://www.valleyclub.co.uk
francis.pickett@cwctv.net

Ryedale Naturist Club

Malton, North Yorkshire
Meeting every other Sunday at the Derwent swimming pool in Norton, naturists can enjoy the pool and sauna without costumes from 4.30pm to 6pm.

There is a clubhouse with licensed bar and self-catering kitchen, used for regular social functions throughout the year. There is a sauna and outside facilities include three miniten and two boules courts.

The club also arranges other naturist activities throughout the year, including moorland walks, barbeques and a caravan rally. The club welcomes visitors.

South Yorkshire Sun Club

Doncaster, South Yorkshire
This small and friendly group of naturists meets weekly to enjoy a naturist swim, and monthly to use the facilities of a leisure centre. Members also organise social events.

Visitors and potential members are welcome and should phone for more details

Valley Club

Harrogate, North Yorkshire
A friendly and welcoming atmosphere greets visitors to this 9-acre members' club, which is set amid beautiful Yorkshire countryside.

There is a clubhouse with licensed bar and self-catering kitchen, used for regular social functions throughout the year. There is a sauna and outside facilities include three miniten and two boules courts.

And if you're looking for the chance to swim as nature intended, the club arranges naturist sessions every Saturday at a local pool during the summer season.

Valley Club, near Harrogate, has 9 acres for back-to-nature relaxation amid beautiful Yorkshire countryside

If you want to bring a caravan or tent, the club has plenty of space for all, and visitors are very welcome with prior arrangement.

White Rose Club

Near York, North Yorkshire

The White Rose Club's naturist facilities are set amidst 11 acres of mature natural woodland. As the club itself says: "Our club is a little piece of heaven where you can retreat from the rigours of daily life."

Convenient for York and the surrounding area, White Rose is proud of its natural setting and woodland walks.

Naturist activity is inevitably based around the heated outdoor swimming pool, surrounded by a terrace and lawns for sunbathing. There is a sauna, children's play area, barbeque, two miniten courts, three boules courts and a volleyball/badminton court. Naturist campers and caravanners are welcome, with prior notice, to use the 16 pitches with hook-ups. Or there are two on-site caravans to hire.

The club welcomes genuine naturist visitors and prospective new members. Contact them first to arrange a visit.

Yorkshire Sun Society

Wawne, near Hull, East Yorkshire

One of the UK's largest clubs, the Yorkshire Sun Society has 26 acres dedicated to naturist activity and relaxation. A combination of parkland and woodland provides the setting for the club's many facilities and social activities.

A heated indoor pool and sauna are at the centre of naturist leisure, while the pavilion has a kitchen and bar for refreshments and meeting other members.

The club also has miniten, boules, volleyball, a children's play area and communal barbeque facilities on offer outside.

Tents and caravans can be brought on site, with two electrical hook-ups available and club caravans to hire.

Naturist visitors are welcome and should contact the club secretary to arrange a visit in advance.

White Rose Club
The secretary, White Rose Club Ltd,
Ashwood, Crosslane, York YO60 7QZ
Tel: 01904 468293
www.whiteroseclub.co.uk

Yorkshire Sun Society
The secretary, YSS, PO Box 795, Hull
HU7 5RA
Tel: 01964 550699
Tel: 07944 645746

Life revolves around the pool at most naturist clubs; picture by Charlie Simonds (www.parafotos.co.uk)

North West

Lakeland Outdoor Club

Millom, Cumbria

A rare treat in the UK, this naturist site actually borders a sandy beach where visitors discreetly swim and sunbathe au naturel. The location's natural beauty and solitude make it ideal for back-to-nature naturism.

However the land is also an SSSI nature reserve which means there are absolutely no facilities other than a tap for water. A neighbouring wind farm provides a reminder that the club's 42 acres of unspoilt grassland and sand dunes are not entirely alone and undeveloped.

The site is suitable for visiting motorhomes, caravans and tents, while day visitors are also welcome. Arrangements should be made in advance.

Lancashire Sun

Near Southport and Preston, Lancashire

Lancashire Sun is a peaceful 10-acre site set in the natural beauty of mature woodland. There are two large clearings for recreation and sport and many sheltered sun traps for sunbathing and relaxation.

For the adventurous or nature-loving, there is a well-maintained path running through the denser woodland. Woodpeckers, owls, hawks, tree creepers and gold-crests are common visitors along with squirrels, rabbits, hedgehogs, pheasants and even the occasional roe deer. The swimming pool is solar-heated and has a warm shower on the pool side.

The swimming pool area has a modern decked area complete with patio furniture and parasols for dining or sitting in the shade while the children swim.

Other sporting facilities include a full-sized tennis court, three hard surfaced miniten courts and a four-piste petanque court. The club had plans to open a sauna and a full-sized volleyball court in 2005.

Visitors and members with small children can enjoy the purpose-built play area with

Lakeland Outdoor Club
Tel: 01229 821738
www.loc.ic24.net
loc@ic24.net

Lancashire Sun
The Secretary, Hazel Grove, Sandy Lane, Rufford, Ormskirk L40 1SX
Tel: 01704 823323
www.lancashiresun.co.uk
lancashiresun@yahoo.co.uk

Lancashire Sun's pool and lawns are set in picturesque woodland; pictures opposite and below supplied by the club

Liverpool Sun and Air
'Sunnyside', Fox's Bank Lane, Whiston,
Prescot, Merseyside L35 3ST
Tel: 07967 88 44 48
www.liverbared.co.uk
secretary@liverbared.co.uk

swings, see-saw, climbing frame, tree house and a sandpit, plus a trampoline for the older children.

The clubhouse contains a dining and recreation area, with a pool table, tables, chairs and comfortable seating and an equally large area which doubles as a dance floor or an area for table tennis. To the rear is a well-equipped kitchen available to members and guests for self-catering.

Weekends see the main pavilion used for social evenings and regular themed events such as a barbecue, dance evening, folk music night, quiz night or an indoor sports night.

The club is situated between Rufford and Tarleton on the A59, close to Southport and Preston. The site is open all year round to members.

Liverpool Sun and Air

Prescot, near Liverpool, Merseyside
The club's grounds, known as 'Sunnyside', have the handy combination of a rural location that's convenient for the motorway network. The club is owned and cared for by its members, with 10 acres of open land surrounded by a boundary of trees.

There are regular social activities throughout the year, and the club prides itself on its friendliness to visitors. The large centrally heated clubhouse has a changing room, sauna suite and Jacuzzi with modern facilities.

Liverpool Sun and Air, or
'Sunnyside' to the locals, is easily
accessible from much of north-west
England. Picture below right from
Roger Hart, picture below supplied
by the club

There are both members' and catering kitchens, a dance floor/social room, table tennis, darts and pool, plus occasional indoor bowls.

The grounds contain a large outdoor pool, lots of sunbathing areas, plus two miniten courts, boules pitches, a shuffleboard court

and a volleyball court. There is also a large covered barbeque area and, for the children, an outdoor play area and playroom.

Holiday visitors can choose from 10 pitches for caravans or motor homes with electric hook-up, plus plenty of space for tents. Drinking water points lie around the site, and there is a chemical toilet disposal point. Visitors are very welcome with prior notice.

Mancunian Naturist Club

Salford, Greater Manchester

Meeting every week at a local leisure centre hired by the club, naturists can take their pick from three swimming pools, a sauna, steam room and sunbeds.

If any of those work up a thirst, there is a refreshments counter selling hot and cold drinks and a range of snacks. The centre has full wheelchair access, a children's activities room and a large lounge area.

Visitors and prospective members should contact the club to arrange a visit.

Manchester Sun and Air Society

Near Knutsford, Cheshire

Set in 17 acres, the club's site, called Springfield, offers family naturists a tranquil oasis away from the stress of everyday life. The club promises a warm welcome to applicants, whether they are new to naturism or looking to join a club after shedding their clothes on holiday. The club started in 1948 and over the years the grounds have been developed by the members to turn it into the attractive site it is today.

From the wooded perimeter to the landscaped centre there is plenty to delight the eye in the club's setting of mixed woodland.

Mancunian Naturist Club
MNC, PO Box 244, Manchester
M28 3JX
Tel: 07760 188822 (10am to 10pm)
www.mancuniannc.fsnet.co.uk
enquiries@mancuniannc.fsnet.co.uk

Manchester Sun and Air Society
Tel: 07821 805866
www.msas.org
info@msas.org

- Camping and caravanning
- Electric hook-ups
- Two modern toilet/shower blocks
- Boules court
- Miniten court
- Badminton court
- Internet/email access

Manchester Sun & Air Society

Family naturism in beautiful Cheshire
New members and visitors welcome

Manchester Sun & Air is set in 17 acres of beautiful Cheshire countryside with woodland walks to feed the ducks. If you feel energetic there is plenty to do on site, and plenty to do and see locally if you want to venture outside. Whether you are visiting with a view to joining or would like to stay for a weekend or holiday you can be assured of a warm welcome.
Web: www.msas.org **Email:** info@msas.org **Tel:** 07821 805 866

- Crown Green bowling
- Table tennis
- Heated outdoor swimming pool
- Children's playground
- Luxury pavilion, catering kitchen
- TV/DVD lounge
- Sauna suite

North Western
Send a stamped addressed envelope to the club: Membership secretary, NWSS, Burnbank, 14b Main Road, Langley, Macclesfield, Cheshire

Many types of birds visit the site including jays, nuthatches, sparrowhawks and wagtails as well as the more common garden species. Squirrels and rabbits look on as naturists walk past and the resident fox often appears as dusk falls. The club also has a number of ponds, to house its ever-growing fish population and resident family of ducks.

Aside from the natural attractions, there is an outdoor heated swimming pool, sunbathing lawns and a new luxury pavilion with fully equipped kitchen, TV lounge and sauna. There is also a barbecue area and pizza oven. Sports include crown green bowling, a boules court, miniten courts, volleyball and badminton, while children can use their large adventure playground. Woodland walks wind around the site.

There are spaces for holidaying naturists, with electric hook-ups for caravans, motor homes and tents. Visitors are very welcome at the club with prior notice.

North Western

Oakgrove, near Macclesfield, Cheshire
A large and peaceful club, North Western lies on a wooded hillside near Macclesfield. In addition to naturists seeking a

The grounds of **North Western** naturist club attract local wildlife as well as peace-loving naturist visitors

place to relax, it counts squirrels, rabbits and deer among its regular visitors.

Stretching over 20 acres, the club is the epitome of back-to-nature naturism with no mains electricity and water rising from a spring. It is among the UK's oldest naturist clubs, dating back to the 1930s, and has occupied its current site for more than half a century.

The members' pavilion has a log burning stove and gas cooking facilities – and the toilets are modern. If you want to stay for a holiday, the site is accessible to smaller campervans, and there is room to pitch tents.

The club has a small membership, leaving plenty of room for everyone to enjoy the peace and quiet. Several terraces for sunbathing, a barbeque area and a boules pitch and miniten court enhance the site's natural attractions. Paths wind into the deciduous woodlands.

Visitors and potential members are very welcome but you'll need to contact the club first and get directions. The club is handy for several towns and cities in the area.

Ribble Valley Club

Blackburn, Lancashire

Lying at the heart of the beautiful Ribble valley, this 4-acre site has been a naturist haven for more than 50 years. Owned by its members and with easy access to both the motorway and public transport, Ribble Valley prides itself on creating a friendly atmosphere for naturists.

There is a large clubhouse with kitchen, evening licensed bar area, snooker, table tennis and darts. Other facilities include an indoor pool and sauna, miniten, volleyball,

Ribble Valley Club
The secretary, Ribble Valley Club, 'Briarwood', Ribchester Road, Clayton-le-Dale, Blackburn, Lancs BB1 9EY
Tel: 01254 878845 (weekends)
Tel: 01282 772393 (weekdays)
www.ribblevalleyclub.co.uk
info@ribblevalleyclub.co.uk

Ribble Valley Club members have been developing – and enjoying – their naturist haven for more than 50 years. Pictures supplied by the club

Solway Sun Club
The secretary, Solway Sun Club, 97 Green Lane, Belle Vue, Carlisle, Cumbria CA2 7QE
Tel: 01228 380947 (for membership info)
Tel: 01228 529764 (for visitors)
royoutdoorsman@wightcablenorth.net

Wirral Naturist Club
Chester and Ormskirk: 01942 492977
Stoke Waterworld: 07771 618237
www.wirralnats.org.uk

children's play area, petanque and a barbeque area. And of course there are plenty of clearings amid the club's woodland for sunbathers to relax and enjoy.

Members organise a range of social and sporting events, and welcome visitors and potential members to get in touch. The club has a small area which is suitable for small motor homes, and a camping area for tents, both of which have electric hook-ups.

Solway Sun Club
Carlisle, Cumbria
One of the larger member-owned clubs, Solway has 15 acres of wooded grounds to enjoy as nature intended. Close to Carlisle and easy to reach from the motorway, Solway welcomes visitors and potential members to come and share the space.

Solway has all the usual facilities to complement its natural setting, including an outdoor pool, sunbathing areas, miniten, volleyball and boules. There is a clubhouse and cooking facilities include a barbeque area. A woodland nature trail and a children's play area have also been added.

Holiday facilities include two club caravans for hire and sites for pitching tents. The club does not have a licence for touring caravans but there is an ordinary campsite nearby.

Visitors and potential members are welcome to get in touch. If you join Solway, you will also need to join British Naturism (see details on page 6).

Wirral Naturist Club
Chester, Cheshire
Wirral's naturists are a friendly group who meet most Saturday evenings to swim and socialise at Northgate Arena in Chester. It also holds monthly sauna, steam and spa pool sessions at the Park Pool, Ormskirk. And three times a year it organises highly popular naturist nights at Waterworld in Stoke-on-Trent, attracting nearly 500 naturist visitors.

At Northgate Arena the main leisure pool has a beach end, allowing safe paddling for children and non-swimmers and disabled access. There is also a water slide and sauna and steam room.

If you want to combine a holiday in the historic city of Chester with a swim, there are plenty of places to stay near Northgate Arena. Contact Chester Tourist Information Centre on 01244 402111 for more details.

Visitors are welcome by prior arrangement. Like most naturist clubs, Wirral is unable to admit visitors who turn up without getting in touch first.

Northgate Arena, opposite; not many countries would tell you that costumes are compulsory in a sauna, but members of the **Wirral Naturist Club** don't have to bother. Picture opposite above by Roger Hart, opposite bottom supplied by club

Sauna Etiquette

Sauna/Steam users must have a Sauna/Steam wrist band on at all times.

Costumes Compulsory.

Shower on the way in.

Shower on the way out.

Enjoy your Sauna/Steam.

North East

TANDO

TANDO
Tel: 01670 518339
Tel: 07970 328144
www.tandoclub.org.uk
tandoclub@hotmail.com

Newcastle upon Tyne

It's by the outskirts of a major city and yet on the doorstep of some of Britain's most unspoilt and little known countryside. It's a combination that makes TANDO a perfect place for a short break or naturist holiday in the north of England.

The club is near the junction of the A1 and A69, half an hour from the North Sea ferry terminal and 15 minutes from Newcastle International Airport.

For the past 50 years the members have developed a full range of facilities. It has a warm clubhouse with a sauna suite.

For outdoor naturist recreation there is a pleasantly landscaped woodland site with a variety of sunlit glades and sheltered lawns. One special feature is the extensive naturist walk through the woods, accessed over the club's Golden Jubilee bridge, a place to stroll freely on a winding path for a back-to-nature connection. The club is proud of its natural attractions and garden features.

For the more active, petanque is popular and there is a court for miniten or badminton. A 15-foot splash pool is set up for use in the summer.

"Members will come to discard their clothes and hopefully cares for a time and we welcome those of a like mind," is the club's friendly summary.

TANDO is also involved in organising swimming and sauna events at local leisure facilities in association with other naturists in the region. Contact the club for more information.

Pictures opposite and below: **TANDO** naturist club's landscaped woodland setting gives plenty of space for naturist games and relaxation

Wales

Cleddau Dippers

St David's, Pembrokeshire
This naturist swimming club meets twice a month to enjoy the swimming pool and lounge area without the hassle of soggy costumes.

A tea break during the swimming gives bare bathers a chance to meet or catch up with other members of this friendly club.

Visitors are very welcome with prior notice.

North Wales Naturist Society

Caenarfon, Gwynedd
This naturist swimming club meets twice a month at the local swimming baths. Members gather for a social catch-up in the bar after their swim.

Visitors always welcome; call the club for more information.

Swansea and District Leisure Club

Penyrheol, Gorseinon, West Glamorgan
This group of naturist swimmers meets in the Penyrheol leisure centre from September to May on the second Saturday of each month.

With access to the pool, sauna and steam room from 7.30pm-9.30pm, members and visitors can enjoy a bit of naturist relaxation and exercise. Contact the club in advance if you'd like to know more.

Tything Barn

Milford Haven, Pembrokeshire
A much loved naturist holiday venue, Tything Barn has 23 acres of woodland walks and tidal lagoons. Almost no other naturist facility in the UK offers direct access to seawater bathing and boating, a fact which also attracts many locals to join up for membership.

Equipped with all the normal holiday facilities, Tything Barn also has two badminton courts, volleyball, croquet, boules, a wood barbeque, a hut for socialising and a sun lounge facility.

Holiday visitors have the pick of two

Cleddau Dippers
Tel: 07773 721477
www.cleddaudippers.org.uk
dickwells@btinternet.com

North Wales Naturist Society
Tel: 07932 745897

Swansea and District
Tel: 01792 232517 (evenings before 9pm)

Tything Barn
Joe and June Folder, Tything Barn, West Williamston, Kilgetty, Pembrokeshire SA68 0TN
Tel: 01646 651452

Tything Barn's tidal lagoons offer seawater skinny-dipping, a rare treat among UK naturist clubs. Pictures of the club below and opposite top by Charlie Simonds of naturist film maker Parafotos (www.parafotos.co.uk), bottom opposite by Roy Wilmot

Western Sunfolk
Tel: 01635 40188
www.westernsunfolk.org.uk
westernsunfolk@ntlworld.com

cottages and two timber chalets, each catering for 2 + 2 with their own cooking, showers and other facilities. There are 20 camping pitches with hook-ups for tents, tourers etc.

Visitors are welcome to come for the day and those living nearby or visiting regularly can join up for a year.

Western Sunfolk

South Wales/Wye Valley, near Monmouth, Monmouthshire
Just one hour from Cardiff and Bristol, Western Sunfolk has an attractive 7.5-acre wooded site set in beautiful scenery near the Wye Valley. The club is an ideal base from which to explore the surrounding countryside, which includes spectacular and historical sites such as Tintern Abbey, Symonds Yat, the beautiful Wye Valley and numerous castles.

There are open grassy areas for sunbathing, a children's play area, barbecue and a large new heated outdoor swimming pool. Sports include miniten, boules, volleyball, pool and table tennis. There are numerous woodland walks. Various social events are held including dances, skittles and quiz evenings in the large communal pavilion. There is also a separate teenager's pavilion.

Western Sunfolk is owned and run by the members on a non-profit basis and was founded in 1935. Holiday visitors and members can choose from 16 camping and caravan sites with hook-ups. There are fridges, freezers, hot showers, toilets and washing facilities all free of charge. Visitors can use the cooking facilities in the pavilion. Sites should be booked well in advance.

The club has a strong family ethos with reasonable fees. Members can visit and use all the facilities as often as they like. It also welcomes genuine naturist visitors (couples or families), who should contact the club in advance.

The volleyball court at the beautiful **Western Sunfolk** naturist club, right. Picture supplied by the club. The picture opposite was taken by Mike Robson at **Linhope Spout** in the Cheviot hills, Northumberland, not a naturist venue as such but one of countless quiet places around the UK where discreet bare bathing occurs

www.barebritain.com

Scotland

Forth Country and Camping Club

Haddington, near Edinburgh

This naturist swimming club meets on the first and third Sunday of the month. Facilities at the pool include two swimming pools, a steam room, sauna and games hall. Refreshments are also available. All visitors with a genuine interest in naturism are welcome to the club.

Scottish Outdoor Club

Inchmurrin Island, Loch Lomond

For natural beauty alone the Scottish Outdoor Club is well worth a visit. Anyone with a naturist heart will appreciate the peaceful seclusion of the island, a unique setting for this unique naturist club. Even the ferry crossing is a treat, with a backdrop of magnificent scenery, and the club has 11 acres to enjoy when you get there. There is a miniten court, lawns for sunbathing, a sauna, a barbeque area and a social/games room for dances, table tennis and darts. The club planned a new boules court for 2005.

Forth Country & Camping Club
Tel: 07720 415 958
www.forthnaturists.co.uk
info@forthnaturists.co.uk

Scottish Outdoor Club
Tel: 0141 533 0233
www.scotnaturist.freeservers.com
daveabercr@fsmail.net

Blessed with Europe's largest natural swimming pool, otherwise known as Loch Lomond, the **Scottish Outdoor Club** has one of the most beautifully natural settings for naturism in the world. Pictures supplied by the club

Scottish Outdoor Club Swim
Contact Brian
Tel: 0141 777 8857

Sunnybroom Club
Tel: 01224 697873
erniemck@btinternet.com
sunnybroom@hotmail.com

Tay Valley Sun Club
Tel: 01250 884323

To make the most of a trip, members and visitors can stay in the two-bedroom clubhouse, which has a fully equipped kitchen and other facilities. Or if you bring a tent there is space to camp.

It hardly needs saying that keen swimmers have plenty to enjoy at the club. Loch Lomond is the UK's largest expanse of fresh water and the biggest natural swimming pool any naturist could wish for.

The club is very welcoming to visitors and potential new members. Do give a week's notice or more for your trip to ensure the club can make arrangements for you. You can also meet club members at their local swim in Glasgow; see details next listing.

Scottish Outdoor Club Swim

Glasgow
Organised by members of the Scottish Outdoor Club, listed above, this group meets to enjoy swimming in water a little warmer than Loch Lomond. Facilities include the pool, a sauna, steam room and hot and warm rooms, all housed in a magnificent Victorian baths building. Meetings take place on Sundays from 9.30am to 1.30pm at the Western Baths in Glasgow.

Sunnybroom Club

Near Alford, 20 miles west of Aberdeen
One of naturism's most northerly, Sunnybroom is a uniquely peaceful club enjoyed by a small membership. Its clubhouse is more than 100 years old and stands in 2.5 acres of quiet grounds.

The club is open from April to October and offers a place to stay or visit for a true back-to-nature experience. Lacking mains electricity, a generator pumps water from a natural spring and powers the lights at night. A wood-burning stove heats the place when the weather is not so good.

The loft in the clubhouse has been converted into two sleeping rooms, with beds provided but not linen. There are cooking facilities with all utensils, a shower and toilets.

Sunnybroom members organise a one-hour swim session on the first Saturday of the month in Aberdeen followed by a theme night and meal at the club. Visitors with or without caravans, motor homes and tents are very welcome, and must arrange all visits a minimum of three days in advance.

Tay Valley Sun Club

Perth, Tayside
This is a small but friendly group of naturists who meet evey two weeks for swimming sessions from October to March. Members also hold other social events to stay in touch throughout the year.

Tay doesn't have its own grounds but offers naturist recreation for people in the area. The club welcomes enquiries from potential visitors, who must be members of British Naturism (see page 6) or other naturist clubs.

St Brides Naturist B&B

Sanquar, Dumfries and Galloway

Not a club as such, but Tom and Elizabeth Carroll offer naturist bed and breakfast accommodation, with optional evening meals, in their private home. They have a sauna and a secluded garden suitable for nude sunbathing. The location is ideal for touring south-west Scotland – Burns country. According to Tom, there are plenty of remote and unvisited areas of countryside nearby, suitable for discreet naturism.

Northern Ireland

Solaqua

Belfast, Northern Ireland

This club organises naturist sessions in the Belfast area. Events include swims, saunas and social activities. Contact the club for more information.

St Brides Naturist B&B
www.stbridesbandb.co.uk
Tel: 01659 50463

Solaqua
PO Box 48, Belfast BT14 8JF
solaquani@hotmail.com

It's not just the Scandinavians who have a penchant for stripping off and enjoying cold water bathing. Many Scottish naturists take the plunge too; picture by Stuart Forbes

General naturist clubs

The Christian Naturist Fellowship

Nationwide religious community

This group was set up by a Christian couple to provide mutual support to Christians who enjoy the naturist lifestyle. They also want to encourage Christians who think they would enjoy naturism but don't know how or whether it is compatible with their faith.

The group has members from every walk of life, including several clergy, and from many Christian denominations. The group publishes a newsletter and a prayer letter and meets in the summer for fellowship and worship for a day in Southampton and for a weekend at the Naturist Foundation in Orpington, Kent.

The club's website has a wealth of information about the Bible's words on nudity and the Christian message in general.

Coast & Country Naturists

Campaigning, recreational and publishing organisation

Coast & Country is a unique organisation, running campaigns about nudity issues and also organising an active naturist club. Based in Scarborough but operating across the UK, its events include rambles, an annual barn dance, a kite day and naturist sessions at many high-quality swimming and spa venues.

The club aims to help more people enjoy naturism and provide top-quality activities for them. The club posts its regular newsletter to anyone who requests it.

Coast & Country was set up in 1982 by naturist couple Sue and David Martin. Initially running a winter swim at a Scarborough school, the group soon started meeting at beaches, forest picnics, photo days and at other club venues.

From its earliest years the group has worked hard to open up the historically closed world of naturism to a wider audience, publishing a holiday guide in 1985 to give both newcomers and experienced naturists a chance to find out more about naturist facilities. It continues to publish a growing number of meticulously researched naturist guidebooks (see page 199 for more details).

While respecting that some members preferred privacy, Sue and David took an open approach to their naturism and started helping beach campaigners and local councillors find out more about the naturist way of life.

The organisation prides itself on helping individual naturists, from simple holiday advice to support for those in trouble with

Christian Naturist Fellowship
www.christiannaturist.org.uk
naturistchaplain@onetel.com

Coast & Country Naturists
David or Sue, Coast & Country Naturists, 3 Mayfield Avenue, Scarborough YO12 6DF
Tel: 0844 414 0146 (local call rates apply)
www.coastandcountrynaturists.org.uk
davidmartin@fsbdial.co.uk

The number of remote places where people enjoy freelance skinny-dipping in the UK are beyond counting, and many naturist groups actively seek out secluded spots to enjoy nature naturally. Pictures opposite from Malcolm and Liann Flight, members of **Suntreckers** camping club. Top Liann enjoys the river Teme near Eastham in Worcestershire; pictures below show remote rivers and countryside in Wales

Singles Outdoor Club
BM-SOC, London WC1N 3XX
www.soc-uk.info
See website for email addresses

Suntreckers
The Membership Secretary, 32 Shafto
Road, Ipswich, Suffolk IP1 5HB
www.suntreckers.co.uk
d-dhoward@ntlworld.com

YBN
www.ybn.org.uk
youth@british-naturism.org.uk

the law. It has taken part in eight legal battles over nudity issues, including the first prosecution under the 1986 Public Order Act, and claims victory in all of them.

In 1997 the club began campaigning over the legal status of genuine naturism. The issue was finally settled in 2003 when the Sexual Offences Bill, which in draft form had threatened naturism, made allowance for bona fide naturist activity.

After more than 20 years C&C continues to campaign and says it never turns away any naturist who needs help. Many members across the UK support the work even though they rarely attend activities.

Singles Outdoor Club
Nationwide members' club
This club makes the most of naturism's social pleasures by providing single men and women with their own group to enjoy site visits, walks and holidays. Founded in 1981, the SOC does not have its own grounds but visits many of the UK's naturist clubs for weekend camping trips. It also organises naturist walks through the English countryside – picking less crowded but highly scenic routes for rambling au naturel.

The membership is mainly men, but there are some women members and the club is actually open to everyone – singles and couples alike. Indeed, the club organises popular naturist swimming nights on six Saturdays a year at Water Meadows in Mansfield, Notts; contact David Broome, the swim organiser, on 0115 986 4626.

Suntreckers Camping and Caravanning Club
National camping club
Suntreckers is a national organisation of naturists who organise camping and caravanning rallies at clubs around the UK. The club is very active, with around 100 events taking place in Britain each year and a growing number of overseas visits.

Facilities depend on which site the club is visiting. It's a members' club so you'll need to join before attending events. Contact the club for more information.

Young British Naturists
For the naturist generation aged 16-30
"It is an exciting time to be a young naturist in the UK," according to the organisers of Young British Naturists. And the club should know, having created a busy and thriving community for younger naturists to enjoy their naturist activities together.

YBN gives people aged 16 to 30 the chance to meet other

young naturists at fun and sociable events held across the UK and in Europe. Members keep themselves busy at events ranging from local swims and weekend visits to clubs to the annual International Naturist Federation youth rally, which takes place in a different country each year.

YBN has a constantly growing membership, with well over 100 participants. It's free to join for any young member of British Naturism (see page 6 for membership details). The club is run by young people for young people and membership is open to singles and couples alike.

All members have a say in where the club visits and what the group does when it gets there – all enabled by the YBN message board, a locked MSN community for members to chat, swap messages and exchange information. There is also a weekly email sent to people containing reminders of events and news concerning the group.

The group has become well-known for its busy and varied diary of activities. Members have the chance to visit a huge variety of naturist places and make a lot of new friends along the way. Contact the club to find out how and why young British naturists are signing up to join in.

Another free-spirited bather enjoys the natural elements in his birthday suit. Picture from Roger Hart

Bare facts

Bare-friendly travel agents in the UK

These travel agents are geared towards the naturist holiday market, offering both fully naturist resorts and regular accommodation close to bare beaches. Remember that bare bathing opportunities can change so it's worth checking when you book.

The main British travel agents also offer resorts with or near bare bathing places but it's not a priority for them so they are less likely to mention them or have current details in their brochures.

Chalfont Holidays
Quality naturist holidays in a choice of European resorts
Tel: 01494 580728
www.chalfontholidays.co.uk

France 4 Naturisme
A range of holidays at French naturist resorts
Tel: 01797 364315
www.france4naturisme.com

Club Holidays
Naturist mobile-home holidays in the South of France
Tel: 01604 863300
www.clubholidays.net

Canarian Dreams International
Bare beach holidays in the Canaries and the Caribbean
Tel: 0870 770 5378
www.canariandreams.com

Don't blush!
These travel agents make their money from bare beach holidays, and expect their customers to want an all-over tan. But if you're speaking to a non-nude travel agent you can always try asking for a room with a sunny balcony that isn't overlooked

Peng Travel
A member of ABTA that has sold naturist holidays for more than 30 years
Tel: 0845 345 8345
www.pengtravel.co.uk

Island Seekers
Holidays on Lanzarote and Fuerteventura for bare bathers
Tel: 0870 112 0555
www.islandseekers.co.uk

Sunseekers
Wide range of quality self-catering properties on Fuerteventura
Tel: 01403 891495
www.sunseekerholidays.com

Astbury Formentera
Specialises in self-catering apartments on Formentera in the Balearics
Tel: 01642 210163
www.formentera.co.uk

It's Natural
Self-catering naturist accommodation at Vera Playa, Almeria
Tel: 01354 661511
www.its-natural.net

Away with Dune
Worldwide naturist holidays, specialises in escorted trips to Crete
Tel: 0870 751 8866
www.dune.uk.com

AV Travel
Naturist-friendly holidays to France, the Canaries and the Caribbean
Tel: 01305 767777
www.avtravel.co.uk

Internaturally Travel
US based company for worldwide nudist holidays and resorts, also publishers of quarterly naturist travel magazine – see website for details
Tel: 001 973 697 8099
www.internaturally.com

If you're making a holiday around your beach or club trip, the following organisations are useful sources of information about what to do and how to get there

National tourist boards

Visit Britain
www.visitbritain.com

Sea Britain
www.seabritain.com

Vist England
www.visitengland.com

Visit Scotland
www.visitscotland.com

Visit Wales
www.visitwales.com

Tourism Ireland
www.ireland.ie

English regional tourist boards

South West England
www.visitsouthwest.co.uk

South East England
www.visitsoutheastengland.com

East of England
www.visiteastofengland.com

Yorkshire
www.yorkshirevisitor.com

Northumbria
www.visitnorthumbria.com

Cumbria
www.golakes.co.uk

North West England
www.visitnorthwest.com

Heart of England
www.visitheartofengland.com

Countryside tourist information

National Parks
www.anpa.gov.uk

National Trust
www.nationaltrust.org.uk

English Heritage
www.english-heritage.org.uk

English Nature
www.english-nature.org.uk

Areas of Outstanding Natural Beauty
www.aonb.org.uk

Forestry Commision
www.forestry.gov.uk

Good Beach Guide
www.goodbeachguide.co.uk

Walking Britain
www.walkingbritain.co.uk

Weather and tide information

Weather forecasts
www.bbc.co.uk/weather

Tide timetables
www.bbc.co.uk/weather/coast/tides

Journey planning

Transport Direct
www.transportdirect.com

AA route planning
www.theaa.com

RAC route planning
www.rac.co.uk

Motorway traffic
www.highways.gov.uk

Ordnance Survey
www.ordnancesurvey.co.uk

Street Map UK
www.streetmap.co.uk

National Cycle Network
www.sustrans.org

South West Coast Path
www.swcp.org.uk

Places to stay

National Trust Cottages
www.nationaltrustcottages.co.uk

Landmark Trust
www.landmarktrust.org.uk

Premiere Cottages
www.premiercottages.com

English Country Cottages
www.english-country-cottages.co.uk

Scottish Country Cottages
www.scottish-country-cottages.co.uk

Welsh Country Cottages
www.welshcountrycottages.co.uk

Irish Country Cottages
www.irish-country-cottages.co.uk

Country Holidays
www.country-holidays.co.uk

Rural Retreats
www.ruralretreats.co.uk

Special Escapes
www.special-escapes.co.uk

Late Rooms Hotels
www.laterooms.com

Late Lets Holiday Rentals
www.latelets.com

Bed and Breakfast
www.visitus.co.uk

Forest Holidays
www.forestholidays.co.uk

Caravan Club
www.caravanclub.co.uk

Camping and Caravanning Club
www.campingandcaravanningclub.co.uk

Youth Hostels Association
www.yha.org.uk

Railways, buses and airlines

National Rail
www.nationalrail.co.uk

The Train Line
www.thetrainline.com

National Express
www.nationalexpress.com

Mega Bus
www.megabus.com

Royal Mail Post Bus
www.postbus.royalmail.com

FlyCheapo Low Cost Airlines
www.flycheapo.com

British Airways
www.ba.com

bmi
www.flybmi.com

Aer Lingus
www.aerlingus.com

Bare facts : Naturist reading

British Naturism
30-32 Wycliffe Road
Northampton
NN1 5JF
Tel: 01604 620361
Fax: 01604 230176
www.british-naturism.org.uk

International Naturist Federation
www.inffni.org

Naturist UK FactFile
www.nuff.org.uk

H&E Naturist
Tel: 01405 764206
www.henaturist.co.uk

Naturist Life
Tel: 01797 364315
www.shabden.co.uk

Bare Beaches
See details on page 103 or visit
www.barebeaches.com

Sources of naturist information

British Naturism

The Central Council for British Naturism, more commonly referred to as British Naturism, is the national body for organised naturism in the UK. Actively involved in compiling information for this book, BN lists and promotes more than 150 naturist clubs in the UK and supports the development of further clubs and beaches. See page 6 for more information.

International Naturist Federation

The INF brings together all national naturist organisations from around the world, including British Naturism. It publishes a world handbook of naturist clubs and resorts every two years. Individual members of British Naturism are automatically members of this international body of naturists, and receive a membership card accordingly. Some of the fully naturist resorts listed on pages 104-106 might require a naturist membership card, particularly in France, but a temporary local membership can normally be purchased on arrival if needed.

Naturist UK FactFile

NUFF is an internet resource operated by a group of enthusiasts committed to broadening the range of information freely available to those seeking details of British naturist activities and venues. The site's organisers helped compile up to date information for this book and it is well worth checking the site before making a long trip or visiting a new venue. NUFF also includes overseas trip reports.

H&E Naturist

This retail magazine is published monthly in the UK. 'Health & Efficiency' has a long and venerable history stretching back over more than 100 years of continuous publication. Today it contains up to the minute editorial and features aiming to provide a modern guide for enthusiasts about naturist living and holidays.

Naturist Life

This UK-based naturist magazine is published by Shabden Leisure Circle, the naturist club listed on page 137. It has plenty of travel features plus news about the naturist world in general.

Coast & Country Naturist Publicatons

Established in 1982, this publisher has been producing naturist guidebooks at regular intervals ever since. All books are mailed out in plain white jiffy bags and prices quoted here include postage, correct at the time of going to press.

- Naturist Guide to the British Isles
  David Martin 202 x A4 pages £12.50
- The Nudist Way
  David Martin 210 x A5 pages £9.95
- Naturist Guide to France
  David Martin 264 x A5 pages £12.95
- Naturist Guide to Spain & Portugal & Islands
  David Martin 248 x A5 pages £13.95
- No Shadows Fall
  Autobiography by Mrs Iseult Richardson 192 x A4 pages £9.95
- Living Sculpture
  Phil Vallack 200 x A5 pages £9.95
- Nude as a Newt
  Phil Vallack 200 pages x A5 pages £9.95

Internaturally Inc

This American company is an established naturist travel agency and publisher. The colourful quarterly magazine 'Travel Naturally' features a wide range of informative articles covering worldwide holidays in the buff. Internaturally Inc also acts as a distributor for Lifestyle Press guidebooks in the US.

The Naturist Society

This US-based organisation promotes and lobbies for naturist recreation and also publishes the well-researched Nude & Natural magazine.

Other reading

- Waterlog

As breathtaking as a plunge into a remote mountain loch in February, Roger Deakin's quirky take on the joys of swimming in the wild is an inspiration to any free spirit. Sometimes bathing naked himself on his tour of wild swimming places in Britain, the author delights in seeking out secret rivers, lakes and beaches. Although he prefers solo skinny-dipping to the social gathering of naturists he sometimes encounters, the freedom and joy are enough to inspire any swimmer to abandon chlorinated municipal pools forever.

Coast & Country
3 Mayfield Avenue, Scarborough,
North Yorkshire YO12 6DF Phone
Tel: 08444 140146
www.coastandcountrynaturists.org.uk

Internaturally Inc
Tel: 00 1 973 697 8099
www.internaturally.com

The Naturist Society
www.naturist.com

Waterlog
By Roger Deakin, published by
Vintage in paperback, April 2000

Advertisers in this book

The naturist businesses below offer a range of services relevant to our readership. When you contact one of our advertisers, do remember to mention that you saw their entry in Bare Britain

Page 39	South Hants Country Club
Page 55	Parafotos Film Productions
Page 65	H&E Naturist
Page 95	Eagle Peak
Page 99	Club Holidays
Page 101	Vritomartis Hotel and Bungalows
Page 103	Bare Beaches
Page 105	Chalfont Holidays
Page 106	Firefly Beach Cottages
Page 107	Desert Shadows Inn
Page 111	Sorobon Beach Resort
Page 121	Little Crugwallins
Page 123	Rivendell
Page 125	Southleigh Manor
Page 126	Tara
Page 131	Diogenes
Page 132	Heritage Club
Page 135	The Naturist Foundation
Page 139	South Hants Country Club
Page 147	Broadlands Sun Association
Page 152	Merryhill Leisure
Page 154	Pevors Farm Cottages
Page 173	Manchester Sun and Air

www.barebritain.com